Woodstock Ontario Book 2 in Colour Photos, Saving Our History One Photo at a Time

Photography
by Barbara Raue
2015

Series Name:
Cruising Ontario

Book 126: Woodstock Book 2

Cover photo: 48 Wellington Street, Page 15

Series Name: Cruising Ontario
Saving Our History One Photo at a Time
in colour photos

Books Available in Alphabetical Order:
Aberfoyle, Acton, Alton, Ancaster, Arthur, Aylmer, Ayr, Bloomingdale, Brantford, Burlington, Caledon, Caledonia, Cambridge, Clifford, Conestogo, Delhi, Dorchester to Aylmer, Drayton, Drumbo, Dundas, Eden Mills, Elmira, Elora, Fergus, Guelph, Hagersville, Hamilton, Hanover, Harriston, Hespeler, Jarvis, Kitchener, Linwood, Listowel, London, Lucknow, Mono, Mount Forest, Neustadt, New Hamburg, Niagara-on-the-Lake, Oakville, Orangeville, Orillia, Owen Sound, Palmerston, Peterborough, Port Elgin, Preston, Rockwood, Seaforth, Sheffield, Shelburne, Simcoe, Southampton, St. Jacobs, St. Thomas, Stoney Creek, Stratford, Tillsonburg, Waterdown, Waterford, Waterloo, Wellesley, Wingham

Other Books by Barbara Raue

Coins of Gold

Arrows, Indians and Love

The Life and Times of Barbara
Volume 1: Inventions That Have Enhanced My Life
Volume 2: Entertainment That I Have Enjoyed
Volume 3: East Coast Trips
Volume 4: Olympics Have Always Intrigued Me
Volume 5: Wonders of the World
Volume 6: Caribbean Cruises We Have Enjoyed
Volume 7: Animals
Volume 8: Storms and Other Major Disasters in My Lifetime
Volume 9: Wars, Terrorist Attacks and Major Disasters

The Cromwell Family Book

Laura Secord Discovered

Daddy Where Are You?

Visit Barbara's website to view all of her books
http://barbararaue.ca

Woodstock is located in the heart of South Western Ontario, at the junction of highways 401 and 403, 50 km east of London and 60 km west of Kitchener. Woodstock is the largest municipality in Oxford County, a county known for its rich farmland, and for its dairy and cash crop farming. As well as being "The Dairy Capital of Canada", Woodstock also has a large industrial base, much of which is related to the auto manufacturing industry.

In 1792, Sir John Graves Simcoe became Lieutenant Governor of Upper Canada and made plans for the development of the interior of Upper Canada. To speed development in the sparsely populated interior of the province, Simcoe granted whole townships to land companies who were obligated to bring in settlers.

Settlement began in Woodstock in 1800. The early settlers were American immigrants from New York State. Increased immigration from Great Britain followed in the 1820s and 1830s, including the half pay officers Henry Vansittart and Andrew Drew.

Light Street memorializes A. W. Light, the first of the military officers to arrive in the area. He was a retired colonel, had published several books, and had many ideas and much enthusiasm for the settlement at the west end.

Table of Contents

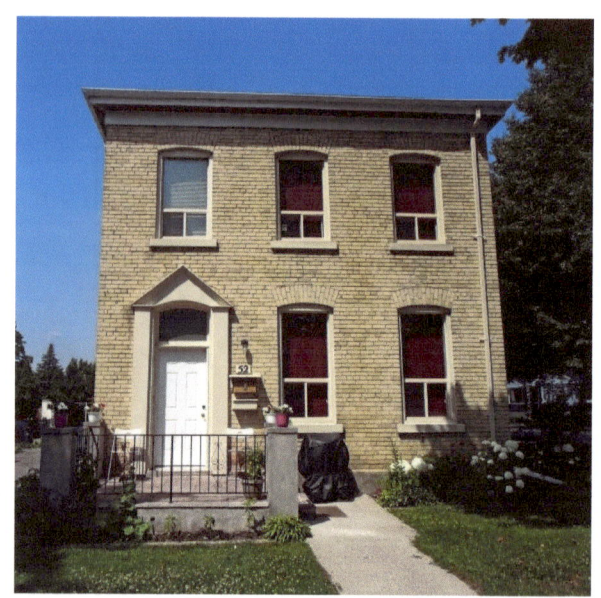

52 Wellington Street – Italianate, hipped roof

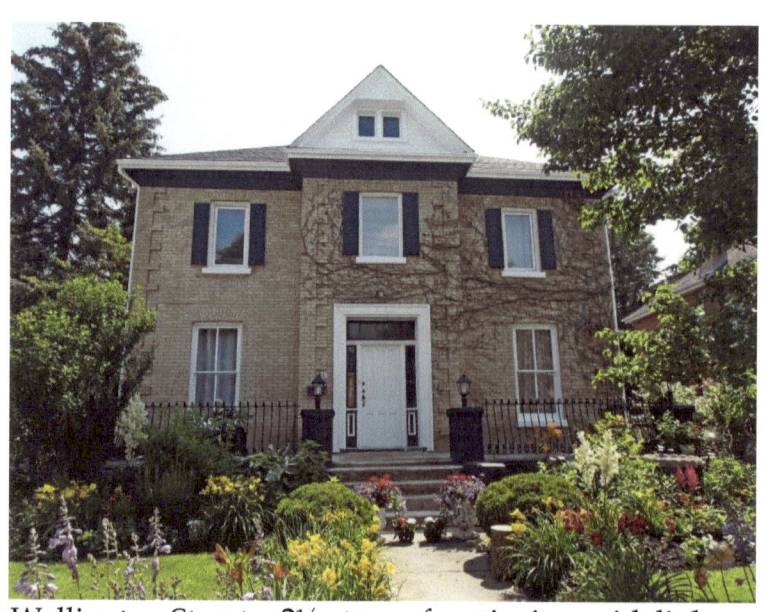

51 Wellington Street – 2½ storey frontispiece, sidelights and transom around front door, corner quoins

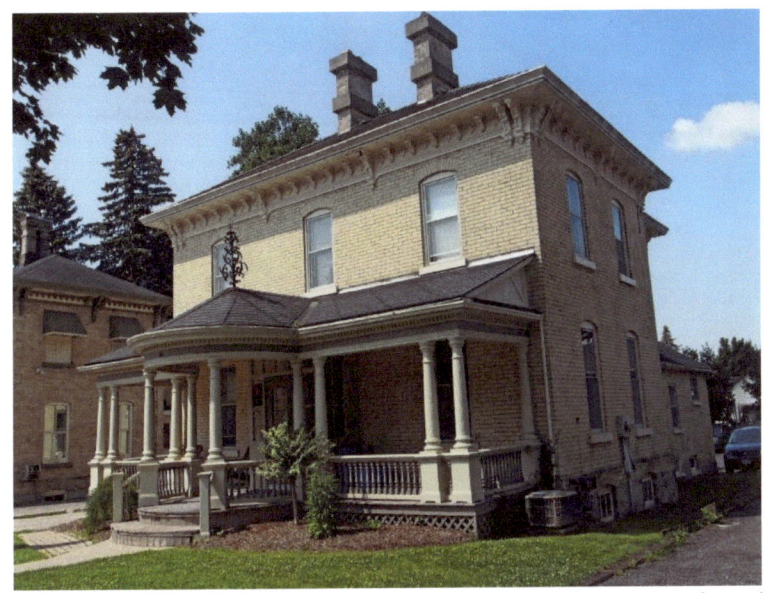

10 Wellington Street – Italianate, hipped roof, cornice brackets, pillared verandah supports, dentil moulding on verandah cornice, spindles on verandah surround

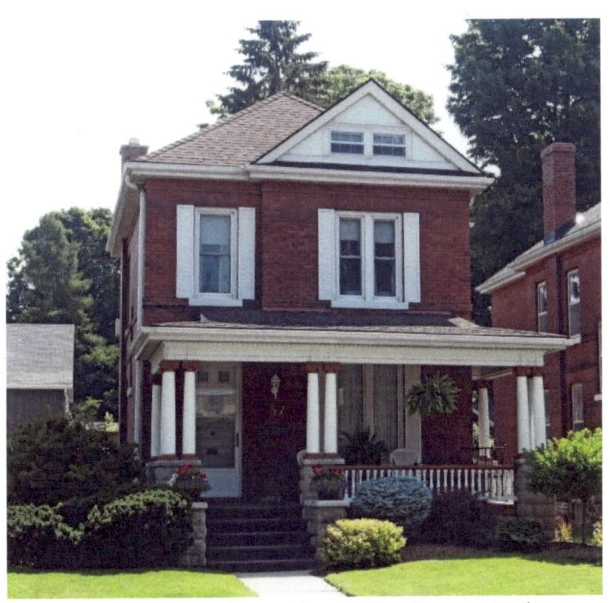

57 Wellington Street – Edwardian, Ionic capitals on verandah pillar supports

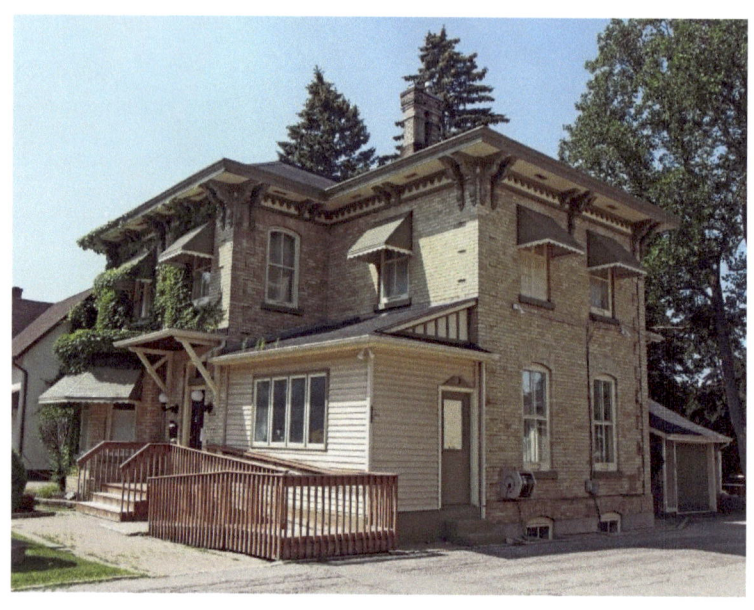

62 Wellington Street – Italianate, cornice brackets, decorative cornice

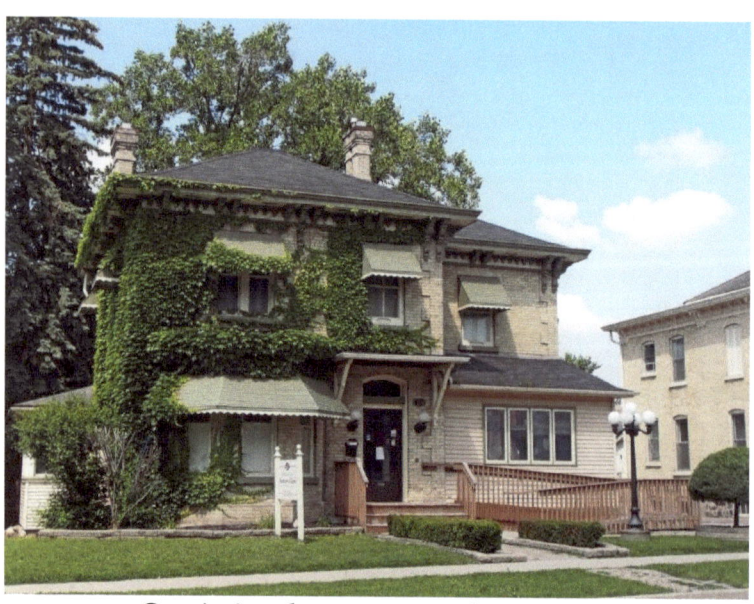

Semi-circular transom above door

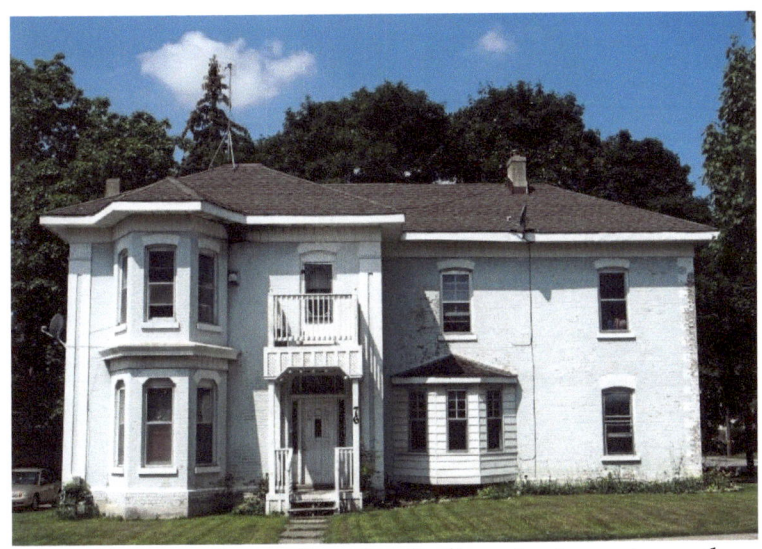

76 Wellington Street South – Italianate, two-storey bay window, balcony on second floor

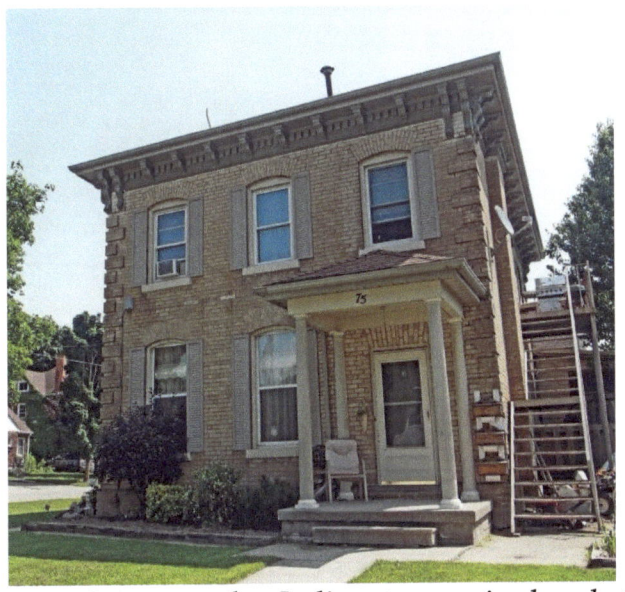

75 Wellington Street south – Italianate, cornice brackets, dentil cornice moulding, Doric capitals on pillared porch supports, corner quoins

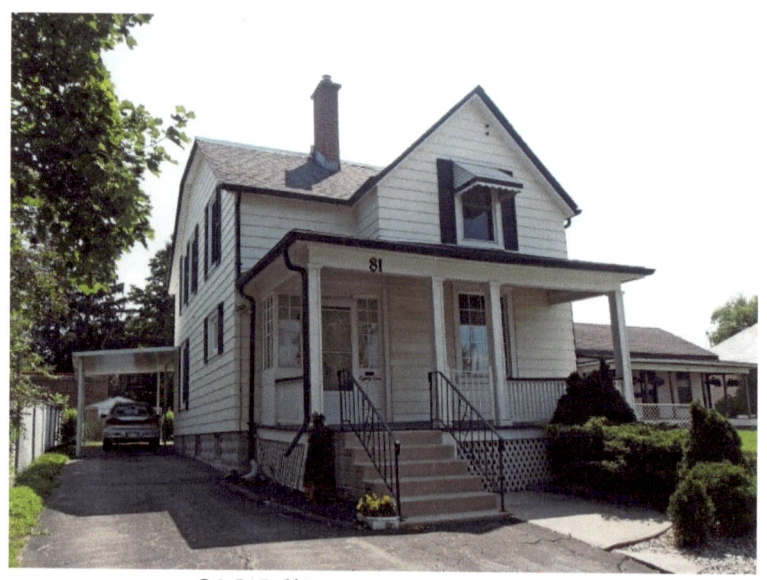

81 Wellington Street South

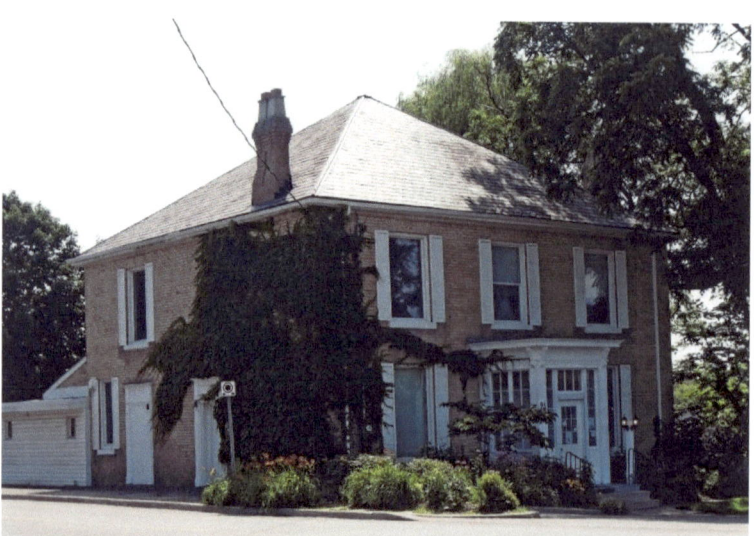

95 Wellington Street South – steeply pitched hip roof, full two-storeys, enclosed entrance with cornice brackets and dentil moulding

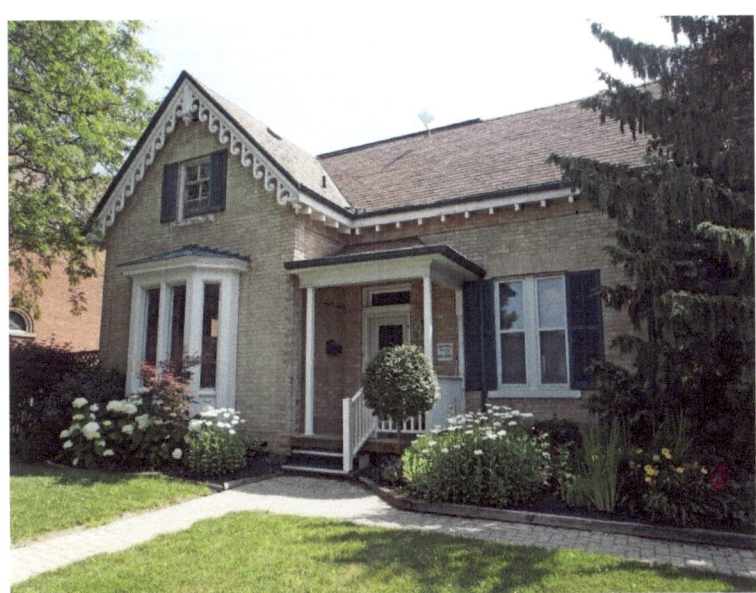

45 Wellington Street South – Ontario Vernacular – L-shaped 1½ storey buff brick, gable roof with verge board with central pendant post

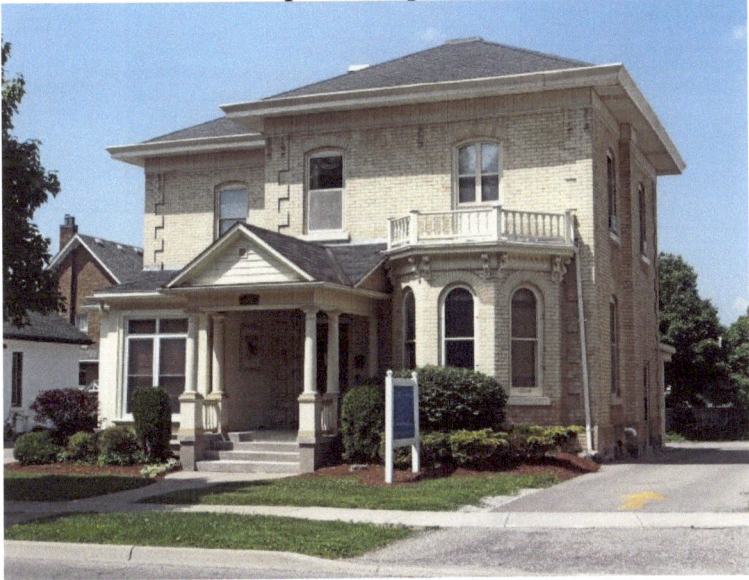

40 Wellington Street South – Italianate, hipped roof, corner quoins, bay window with balcony above, pediment above pillared porch

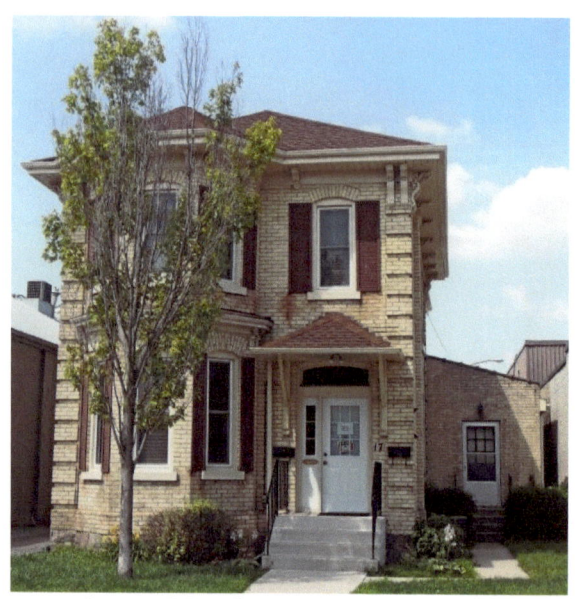

17 Wellington Street North – Italianate, hipped roof, paired cornice brackets, corner quoins, two-storey bay window

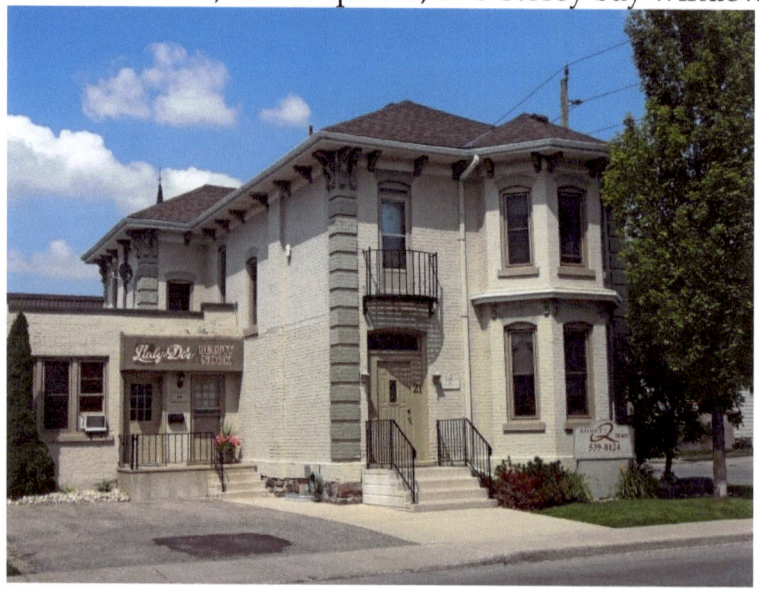

19-21 Wellington Street North – Italianate, single cornice brackets, corner quoins, two-storey bay window, second floor balcony

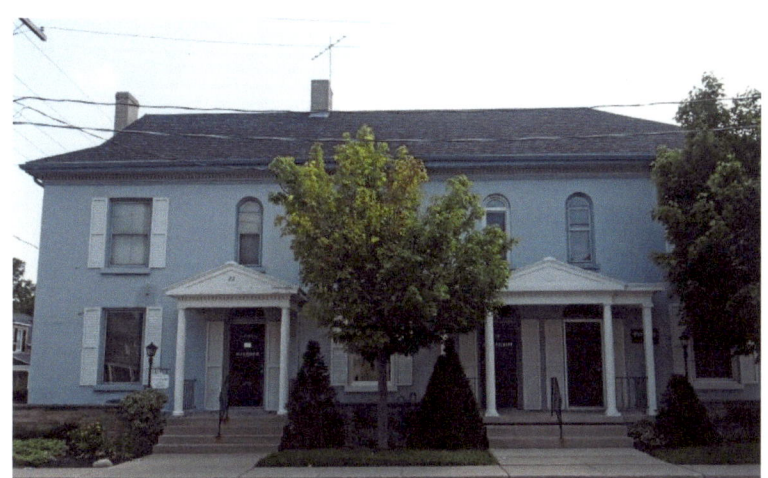

20-22 Wellington Street North – pediments and dentil
moulding above pillared porches

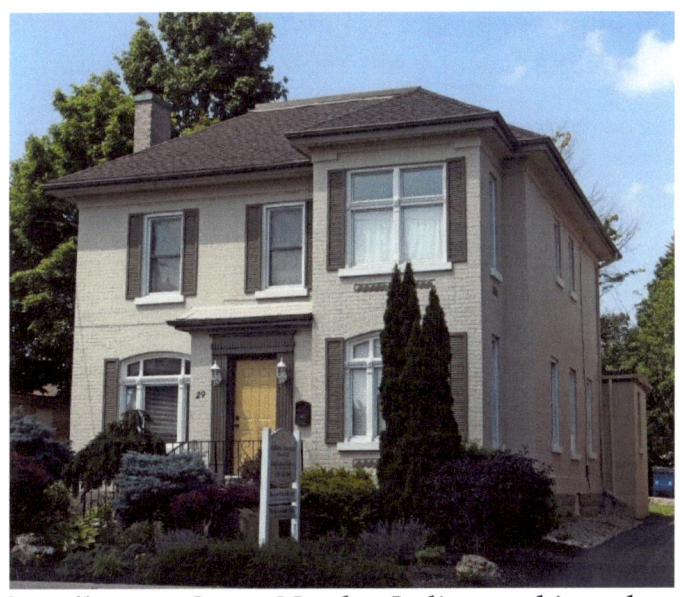

29 Wellington Street North – Italianate, hipped roof

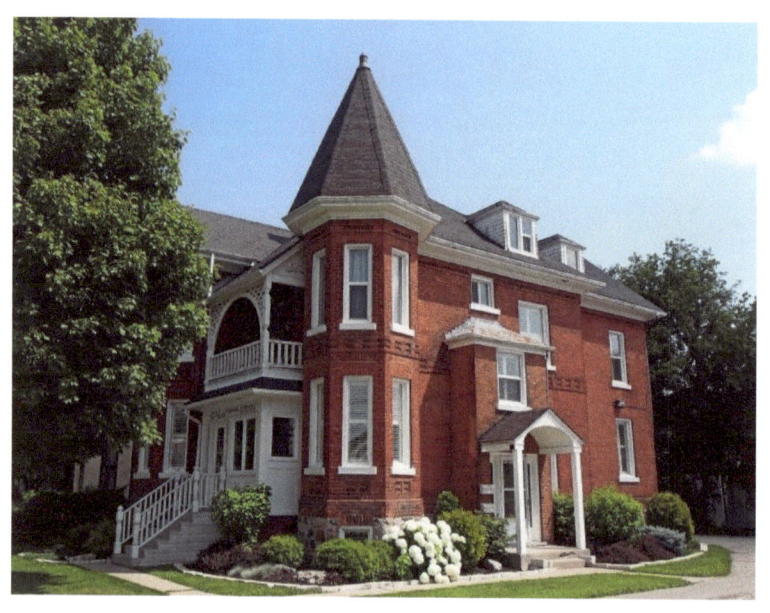

36 Wellington Street North – two storey turret, dormers, second floor balcony with spindle decorative work

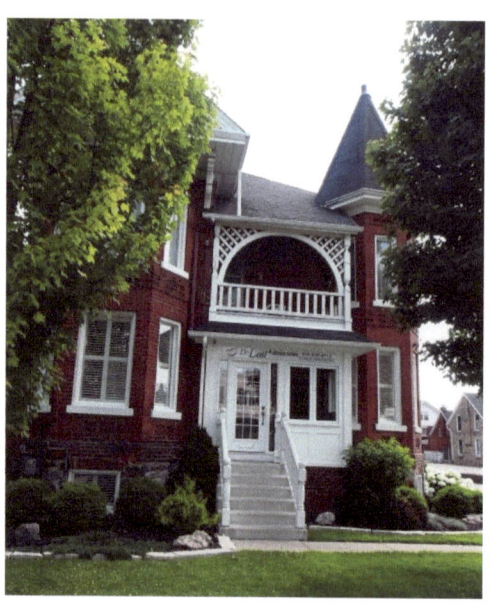

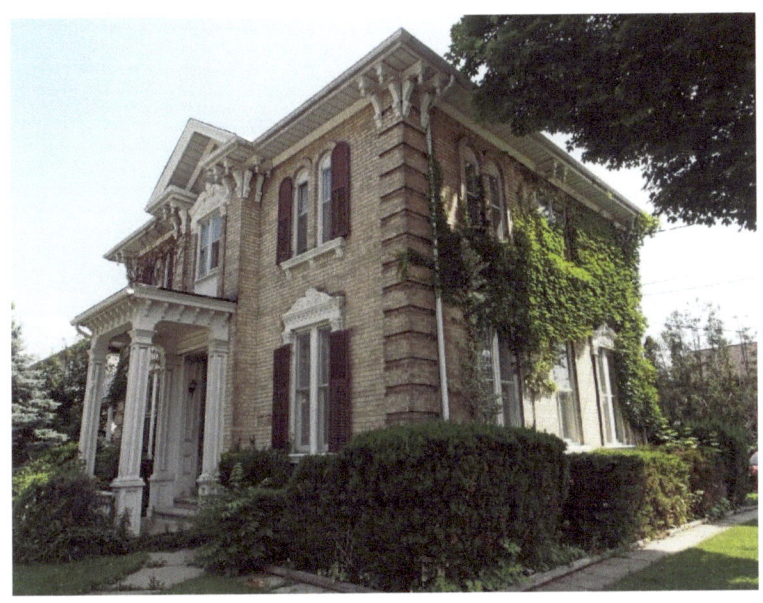

48 Wellington Street – Italianate, hipped roof, paired cornice
brackets, window hoods, corner quoining, entrance

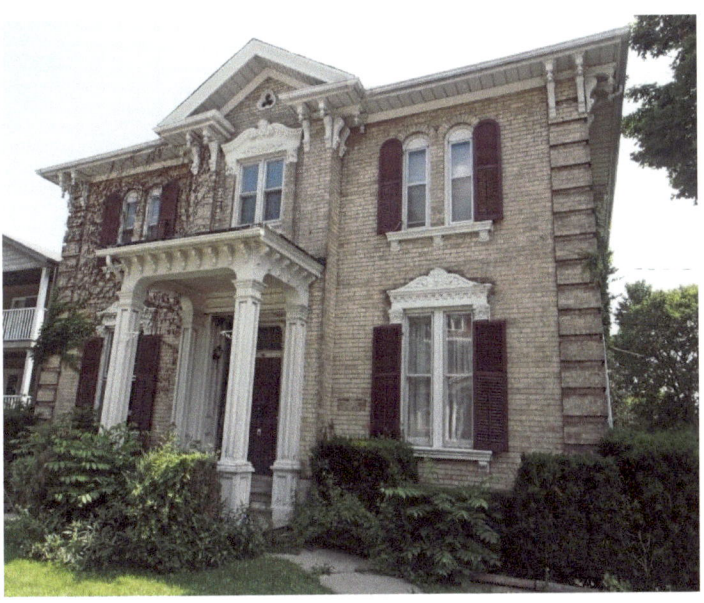

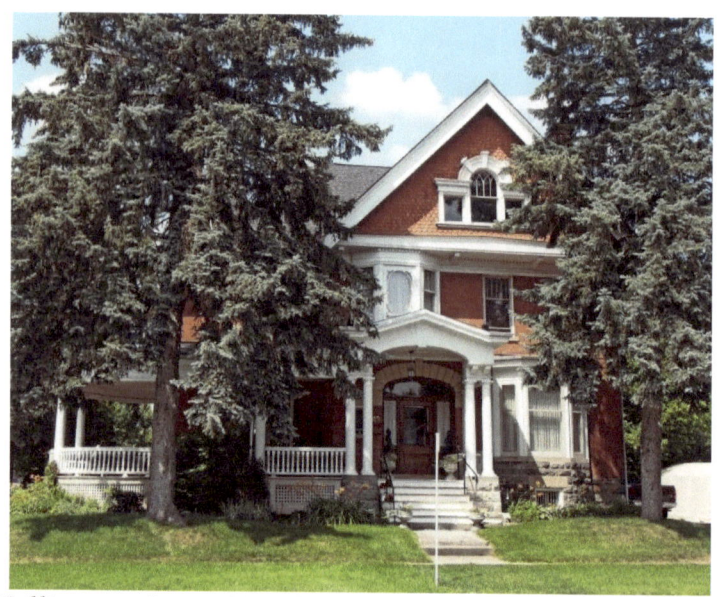

49 Wellington Street North – Edwardian, Palladian window, Doric capitals on pillared supports on wraparound verandah

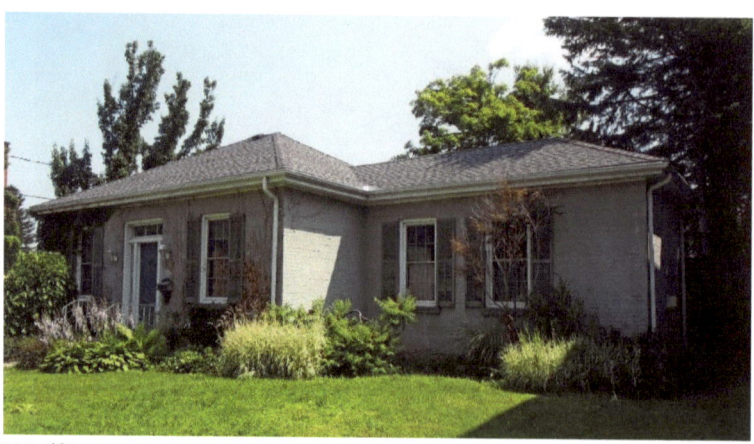

64 Wellington Street – Regency Cottage, one storey, hip roof

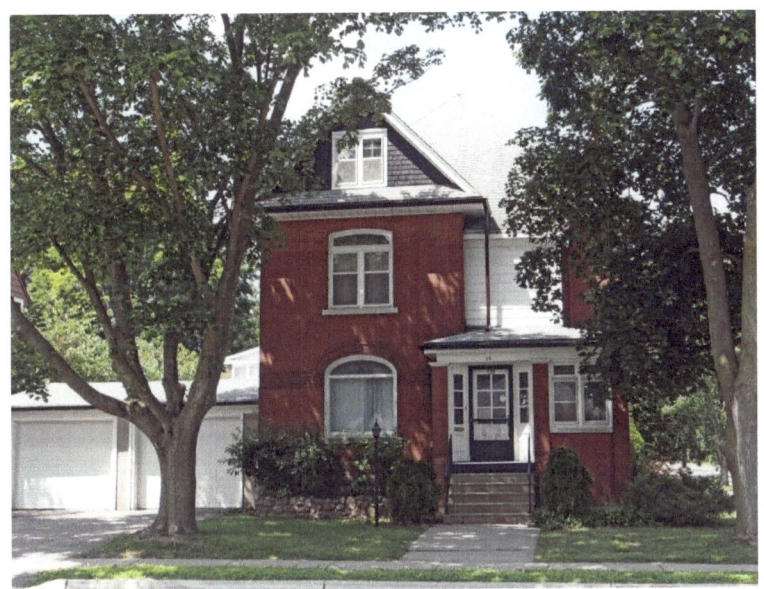

65 Wellington Street - Edwardian

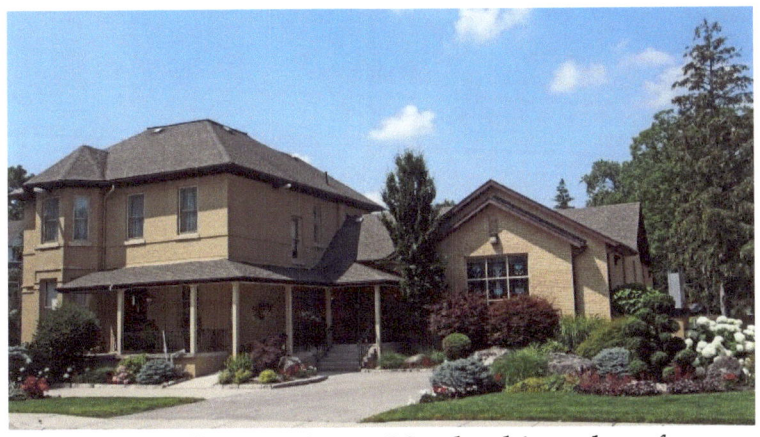

69 Wellington Street North – hipped roof

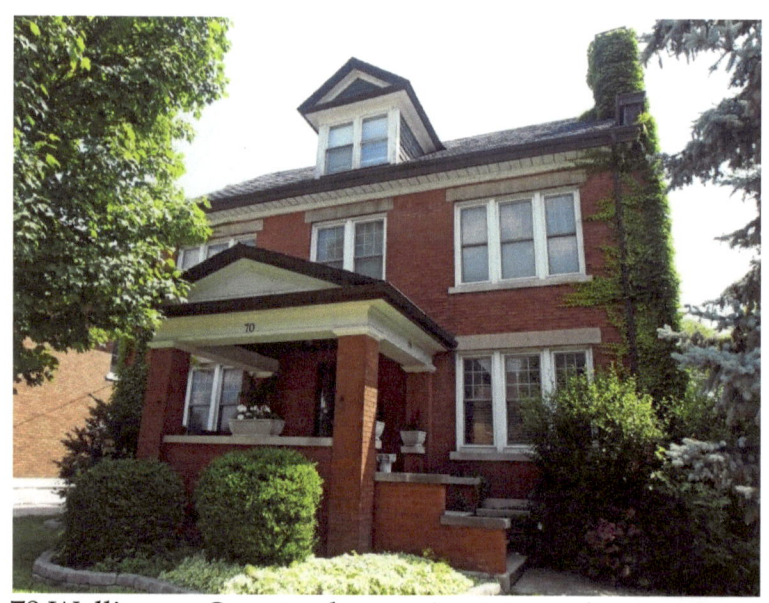

70 Wellington Street – dormer in attic, pediment above verandah

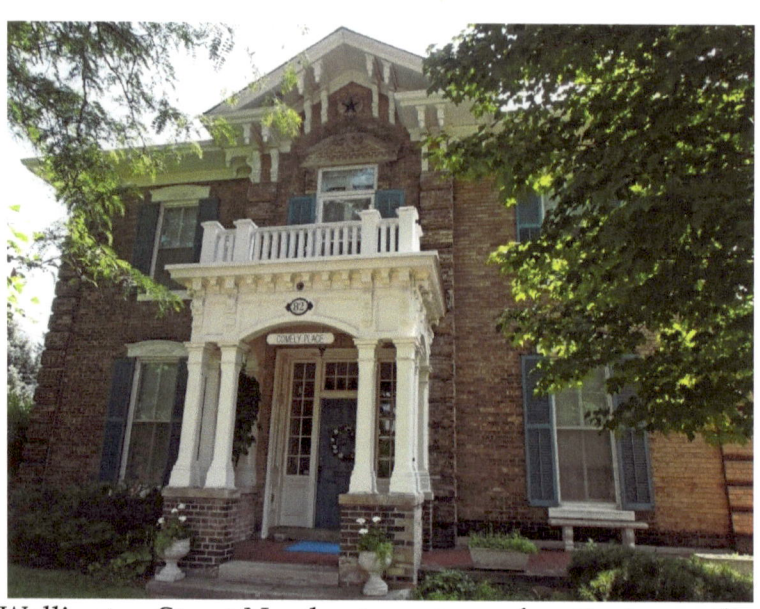

82 Wellington Street North – two-storey frontispiece, pillared entrance with balcony above, corner quoins

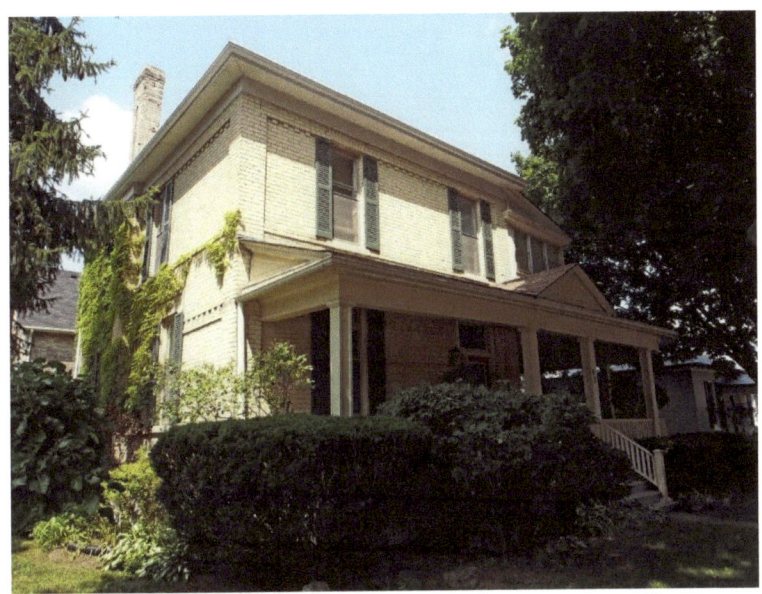

87 Wellington Street North – Italianate - pediment

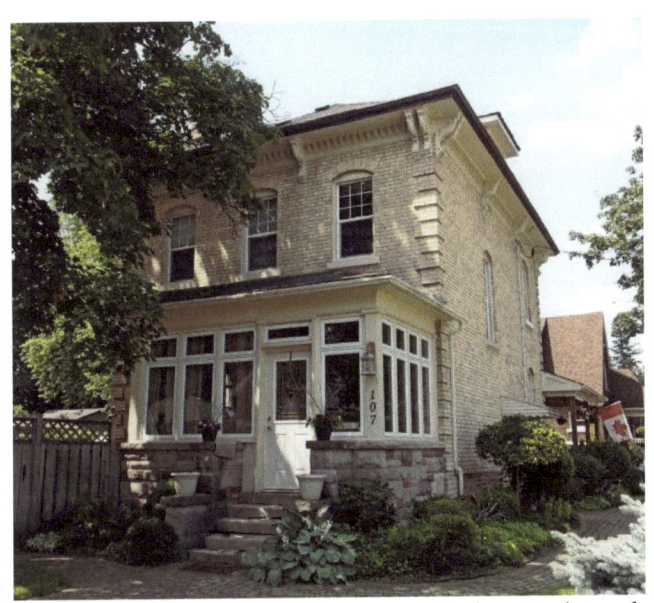

107 Wellington Street North – Italianate, hipped roof, cornice brackets and dentil moulding, corner quoins, enclosed porch

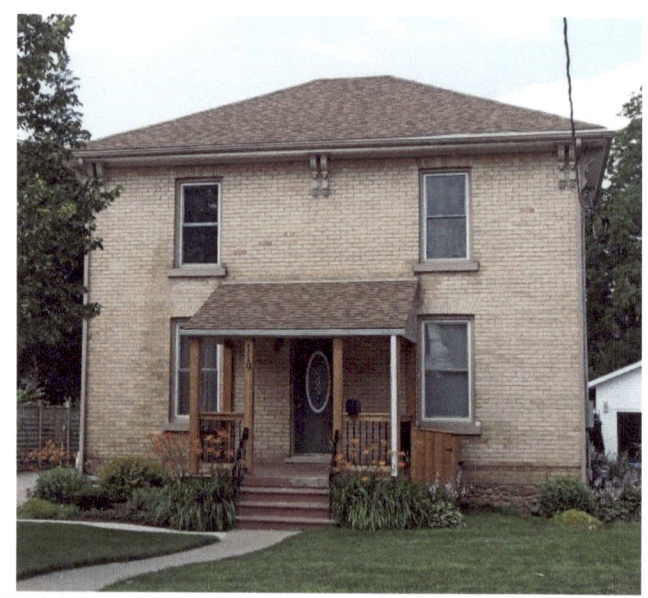

119 Riddell Street – hipped roof, paired cornice brackets

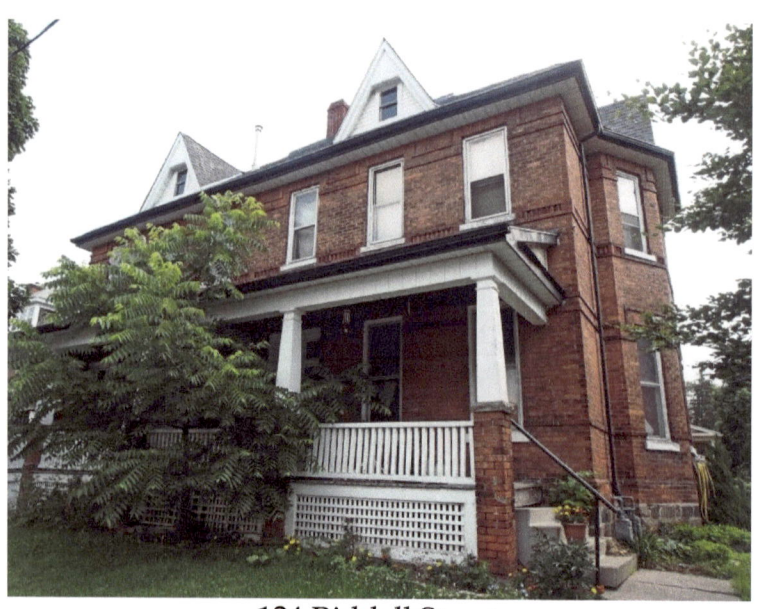

124 Riddell Street

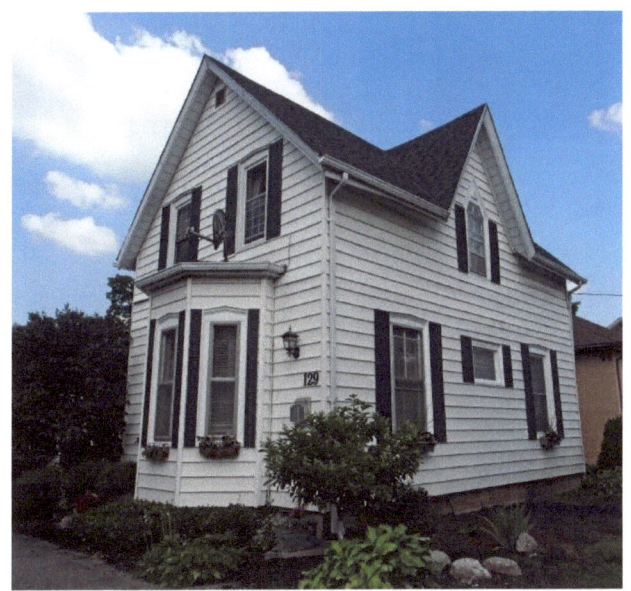

129 Riddell Street – Gothic Revival, bay window

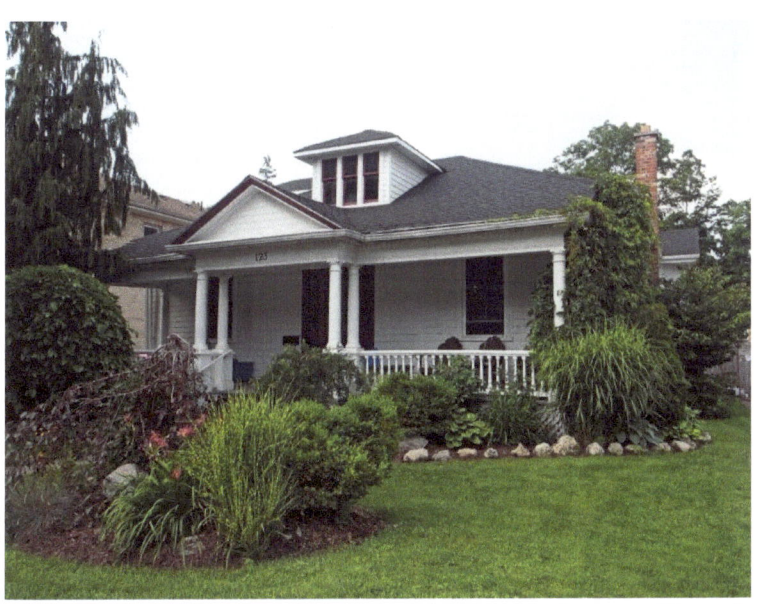

123 Riddell Street – dormer, pediment above pillared verandah

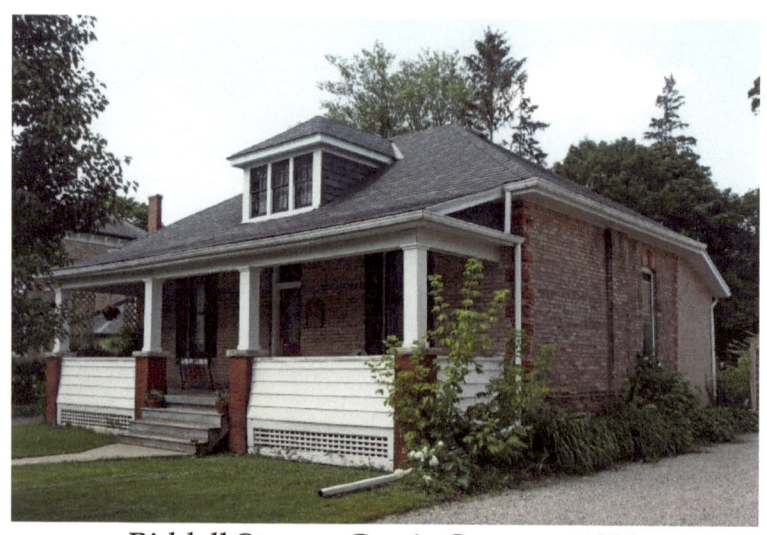

Riddell Street – Currie Cottage - 1890

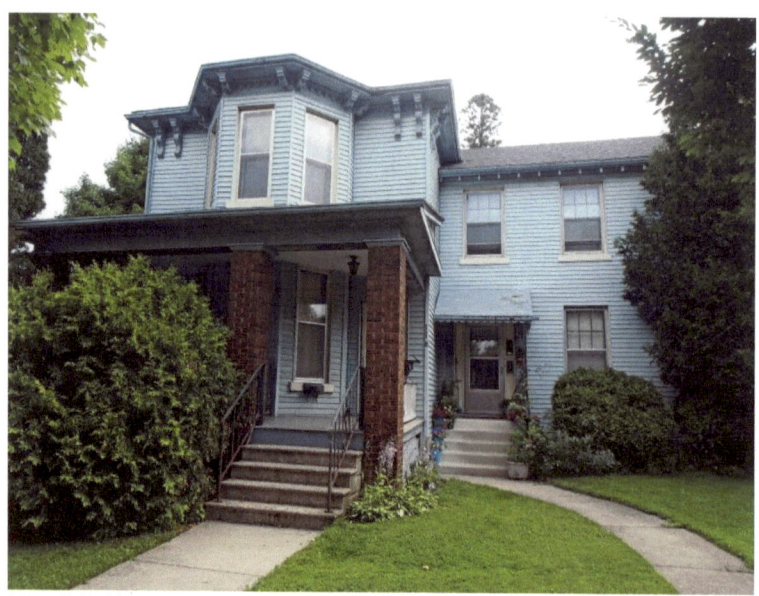

116 Riddell Street – Italianate, cornice brackets, bay window

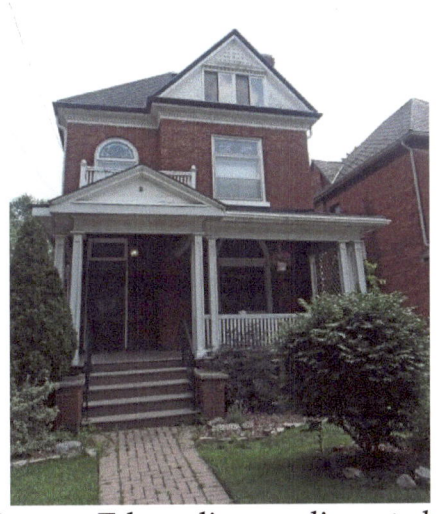

Riddell Street – Edwardian, pediment above door

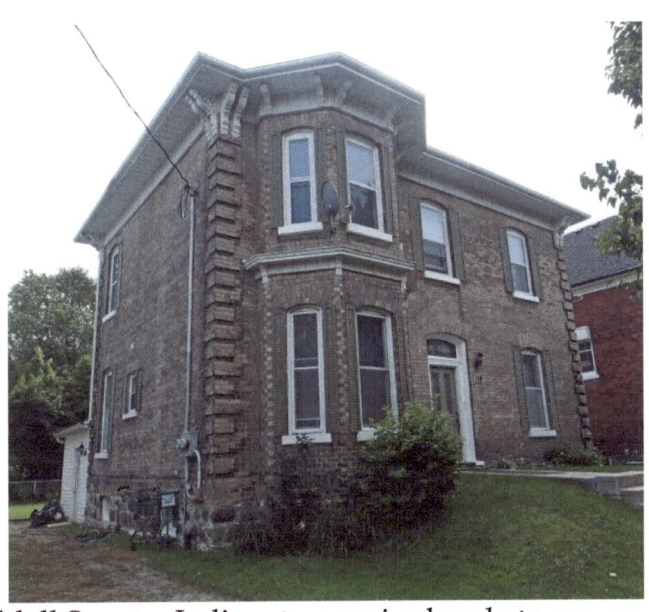

108 Riddell Street – Italianate, cornice brackets, corner quoins,
two-storey tower-like bay

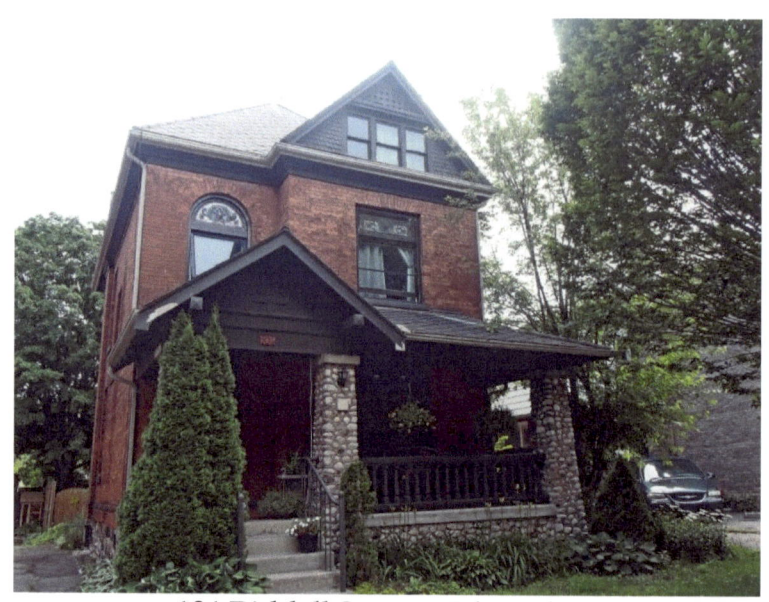

104 Riddell Street - Edwardian

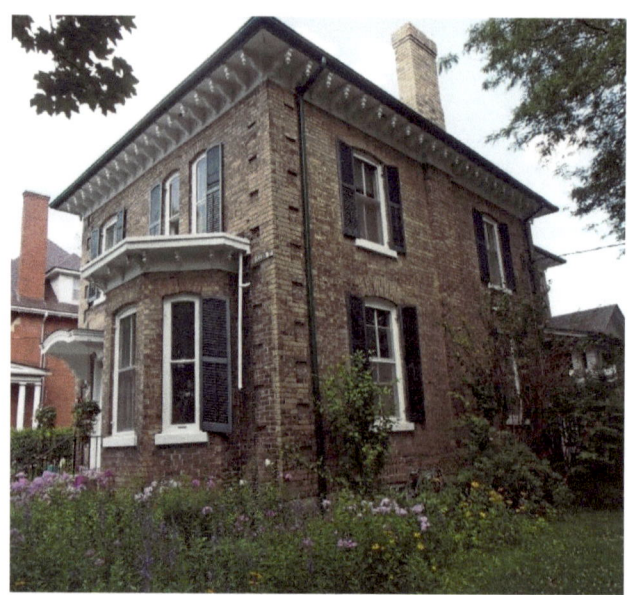

467 Riddell Street – Italianate, cornice brackets, bay window, corner quoins

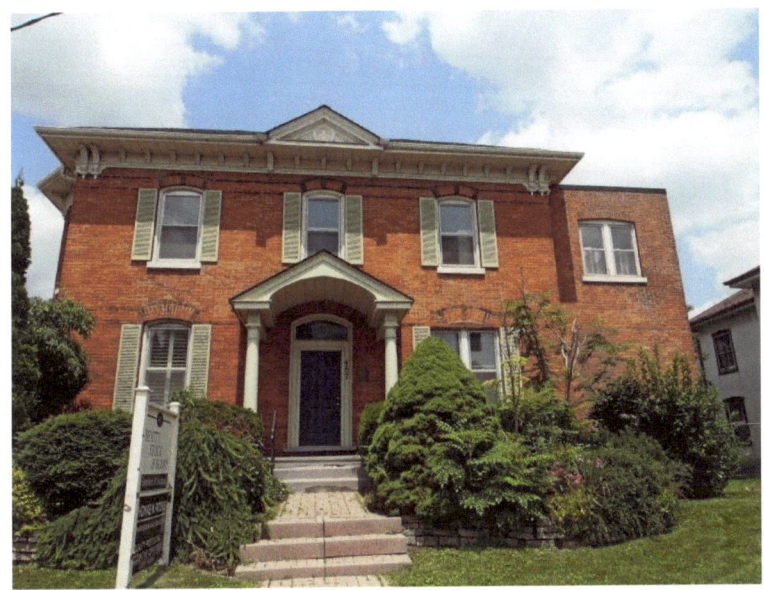

487 Riddell Street – Bickerton House – 1881 – Georgian style, cornice brackets, pediment with decorated tympanum, Doric capitals on pillared porch supports

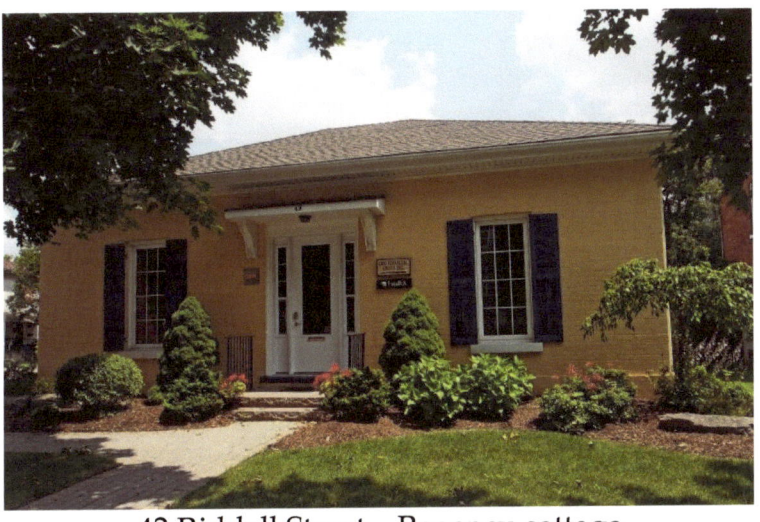

42 Riddell Street – Regency cottage

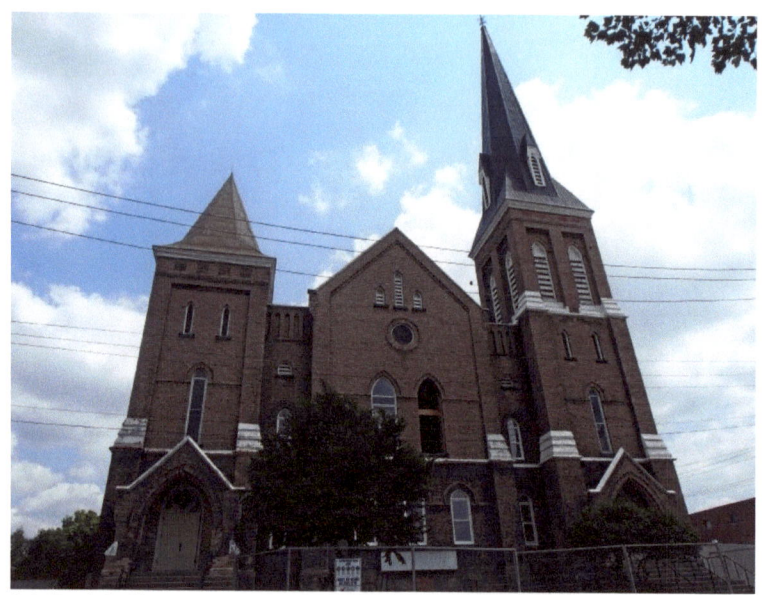

34 Riddell Street – Central United Church built in 1876
Lancet windows, rose window

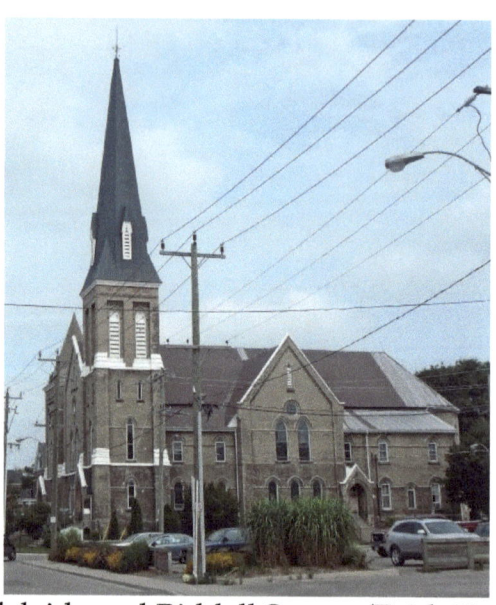

Corner of Adelaide and Riddell Streets (Faith United Church)

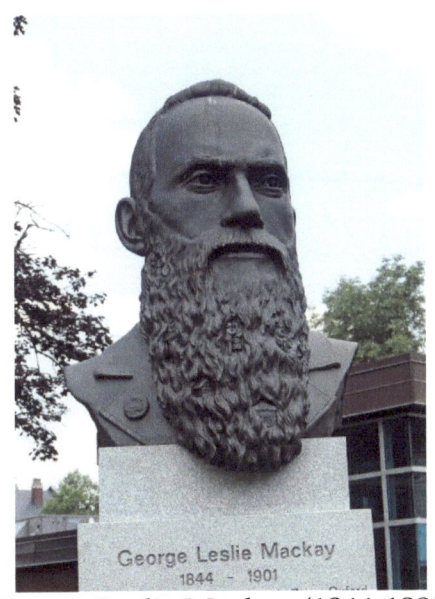

George Leslie Mackay (1844-1901)

He was born in Zorra, Oxford County of Scottish Presbyterian immigrants. In 1872 in Taiwan he founded the first Canadian overseas mission. He was famed for unorthodox yet successful methods, respect for local culture, his Taiwanese wife Tiu Chhang-mia, and his outspoken opposition to Canada's head tax – all ahead of his time. In 1881 churches in Oxford County donated $6,200 to build the first western school in north Taiwan – Oxford College Tamsui. Mackay also built Taiwan's first hospital, women's school, and museum.

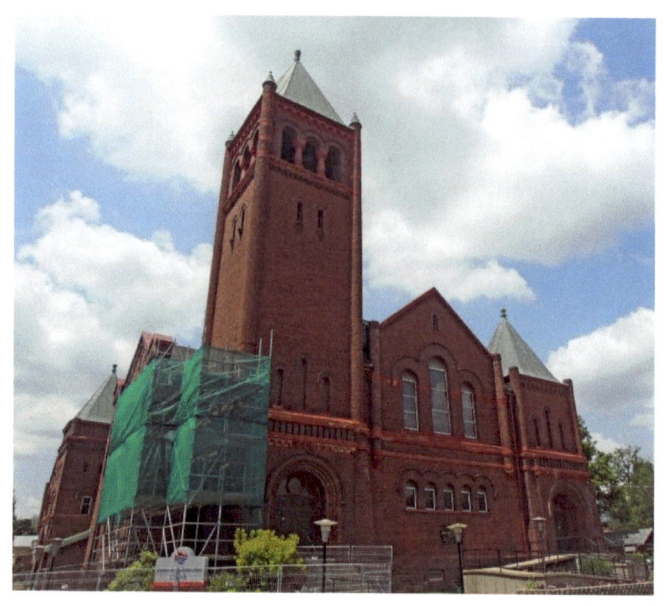

59 Riddell Street – Knox Presbyterian Church

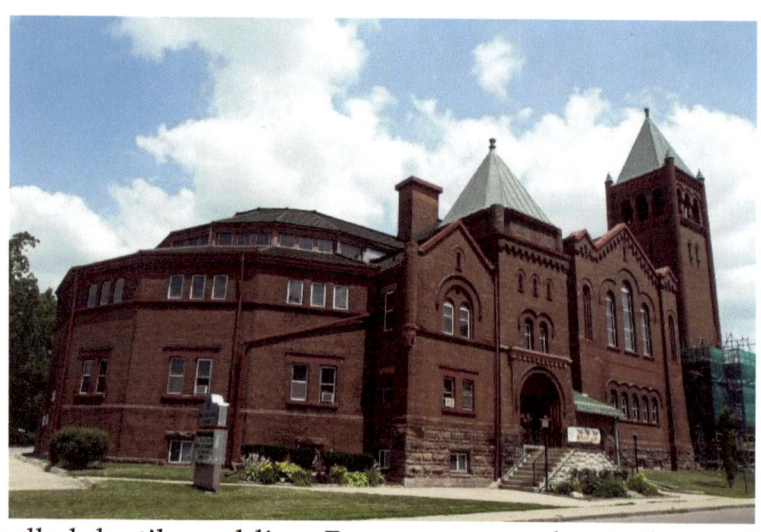

Bevelled dentil moulding, Romanesque style window arches,
banding, finials

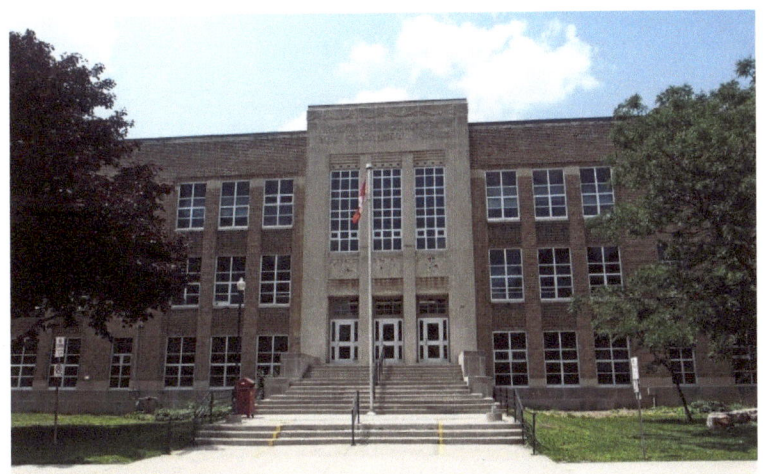

35 Riddell Street – Woodstock Collegiate and Vocational School is known for celebrating excellence in academics, the arts, technology and athletics. "Knowledge, Industry, Character" inscribed above the front doors.

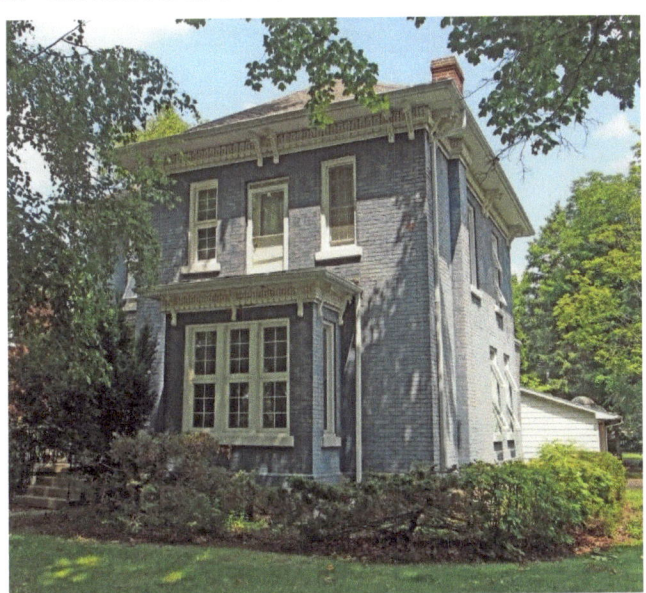

427 Drew Street – Italianate, hipped roof, rectangular bay window, cornice brackets

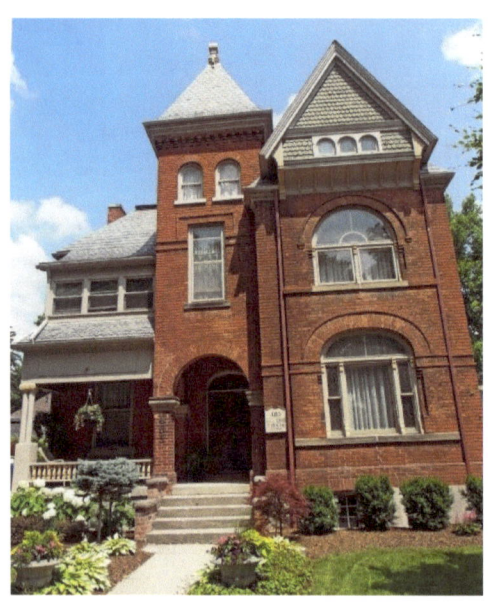

405 Drew Street – c. 1891 – T. McClay, builder - Queen Anne, 2½ storey tower, banding, Romanesque style window arches

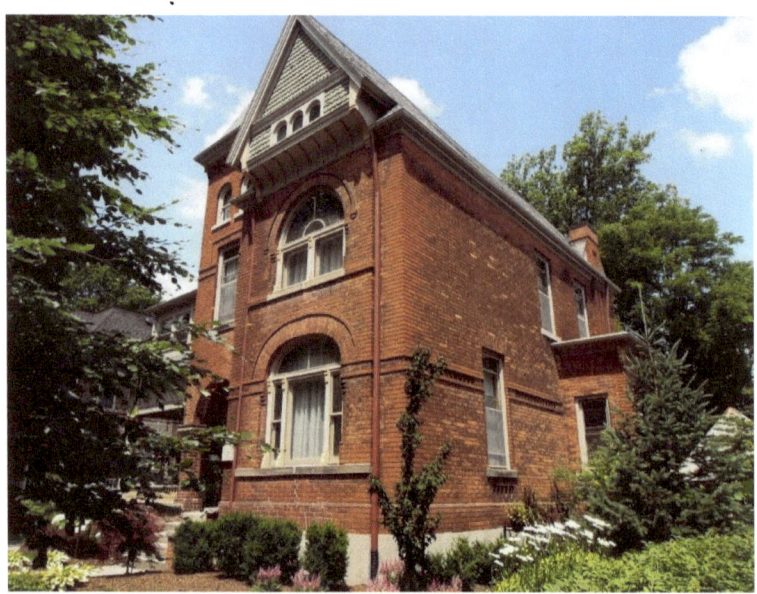

Saw tooth brick detailing

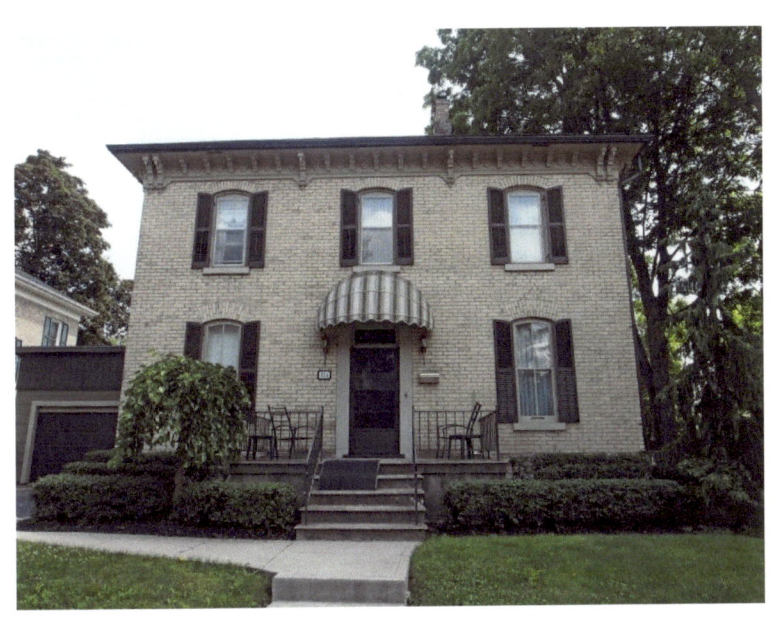

314 Drew Street – Italianate, hipped roof, cornice brackets

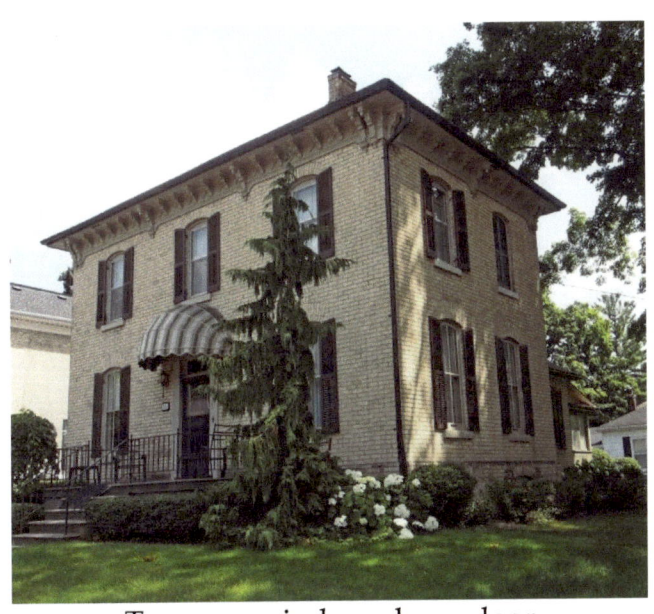

Transom window above door

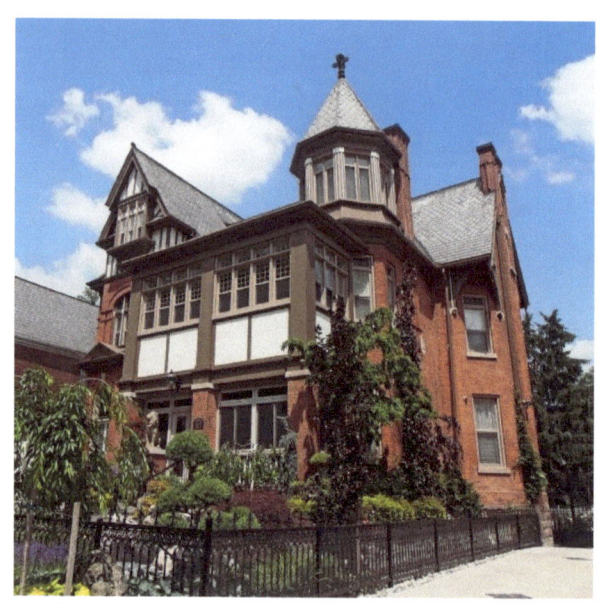

419 Drew Street – Queen Anne – turret, some Tudor style detailing

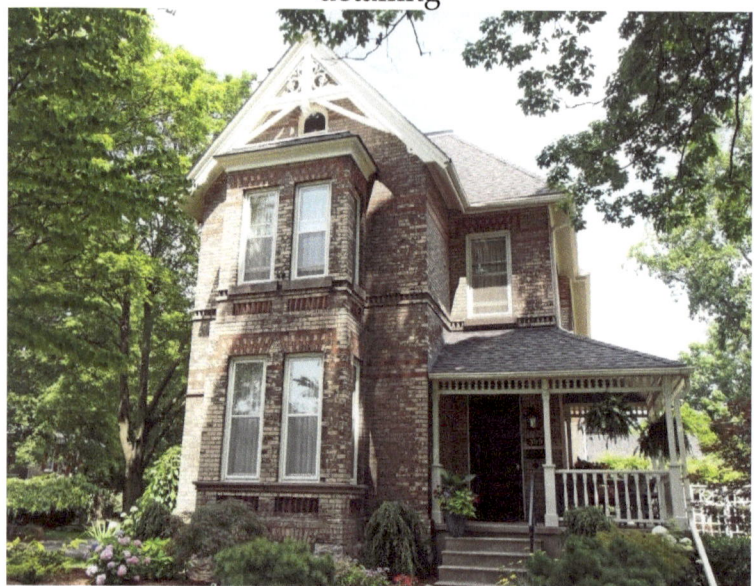

399 Drew Street – dichromatic brickwork, two-storey rectangular bay window, verge board time on gable with finial, saw tooth brickwork, spindle trim on verandah

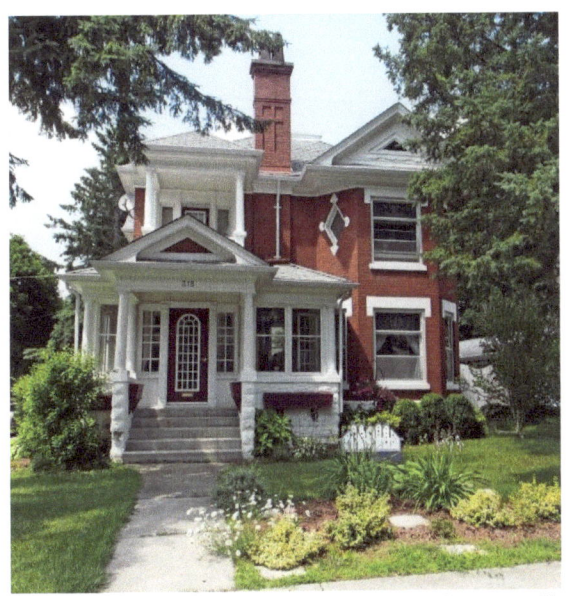

315 Drew Street –sidelights surrounding door, pillared porch supports, pediment with pillared second floor balcony above

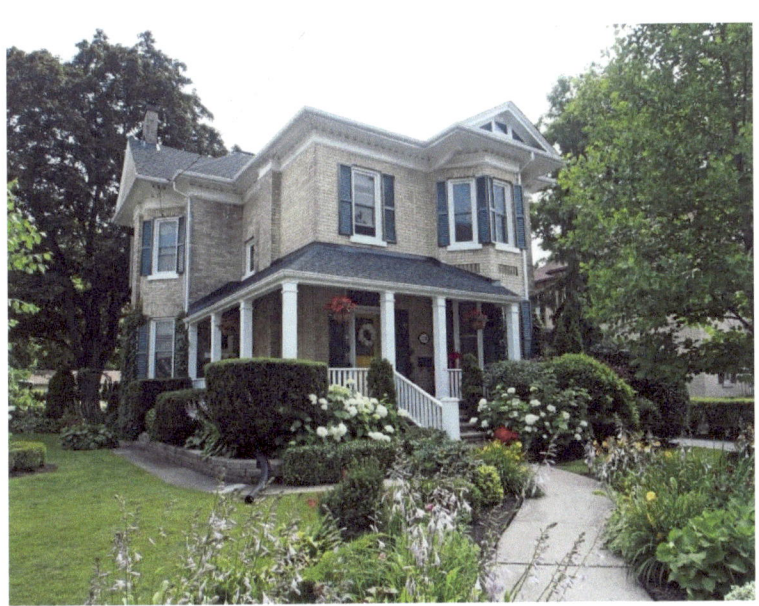

320 Drew Street – two-storey tower like bays, wraparound verandah

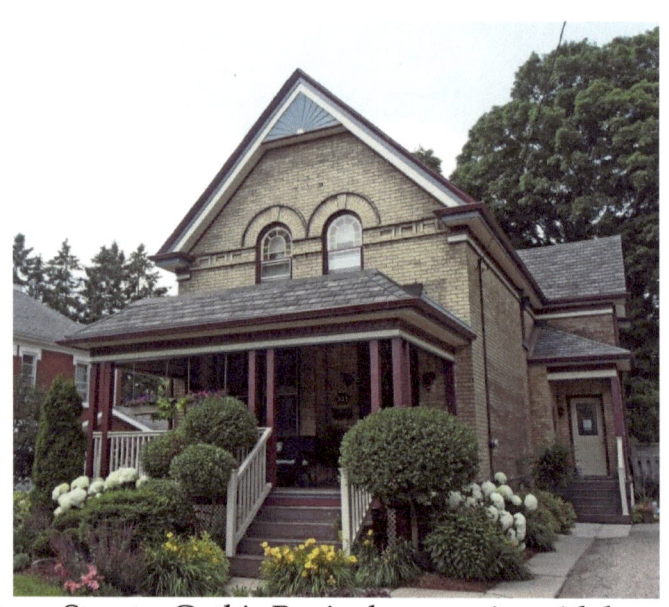

321 Drew Street – Gothic Revival, voussoirs with keystones, sunburst design in gable, decorative brickwork, dentil moulding below porch cornice

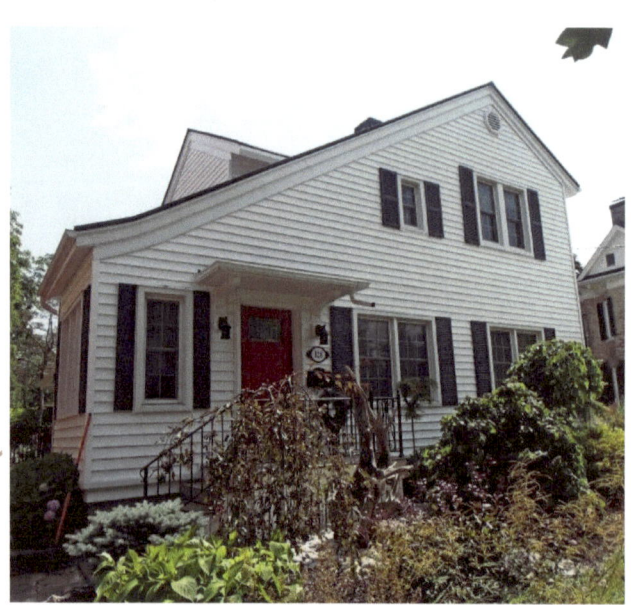

328 Drew Street - Saltbox

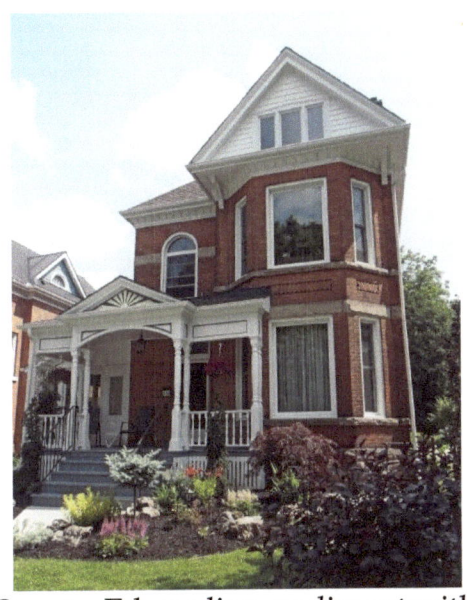

330 Drew Street – Edwardian, pediment with decorated tympanum above porch with turned supports, decorative brickwork

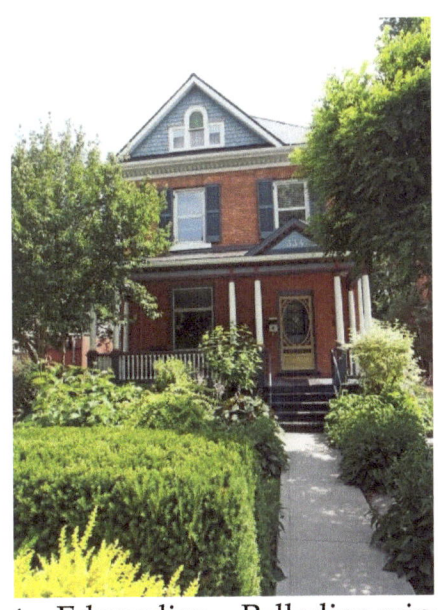

334 Drew Street – Edwardian – Palladian window, pediment

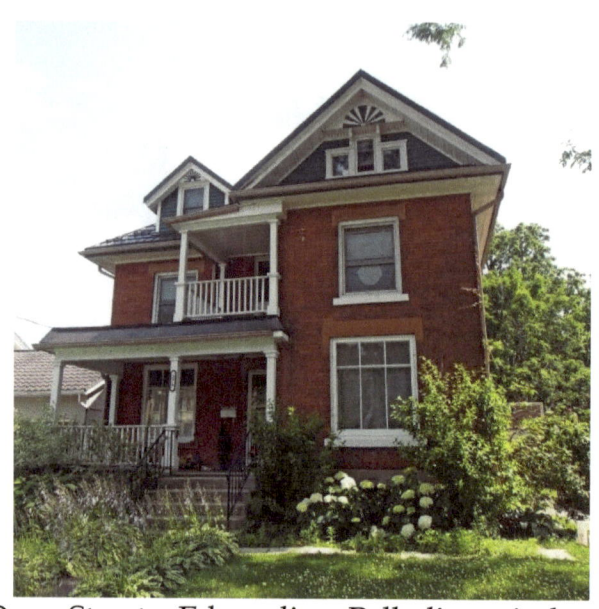

376 Drew Street – Edwardian, Palladian window with sunburst pattern above, second floor balcony, dormer

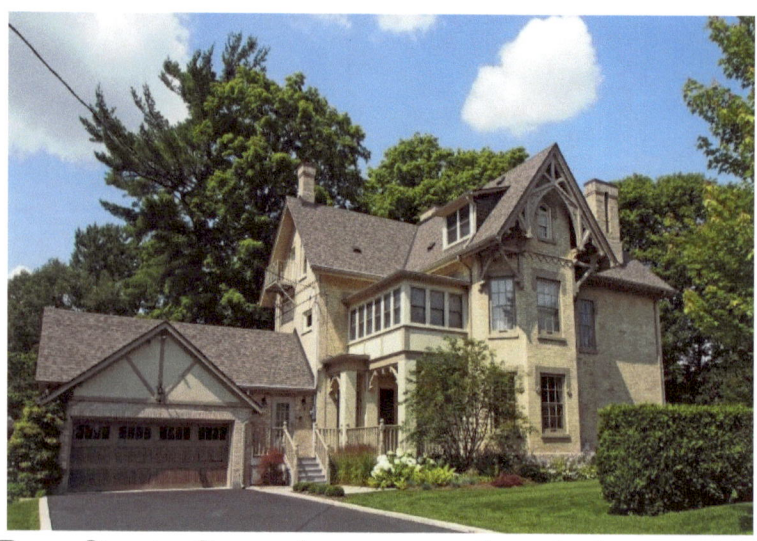

Drew Street – Queen Anne – verge board trim on gable, 2½ storey tower-like bay

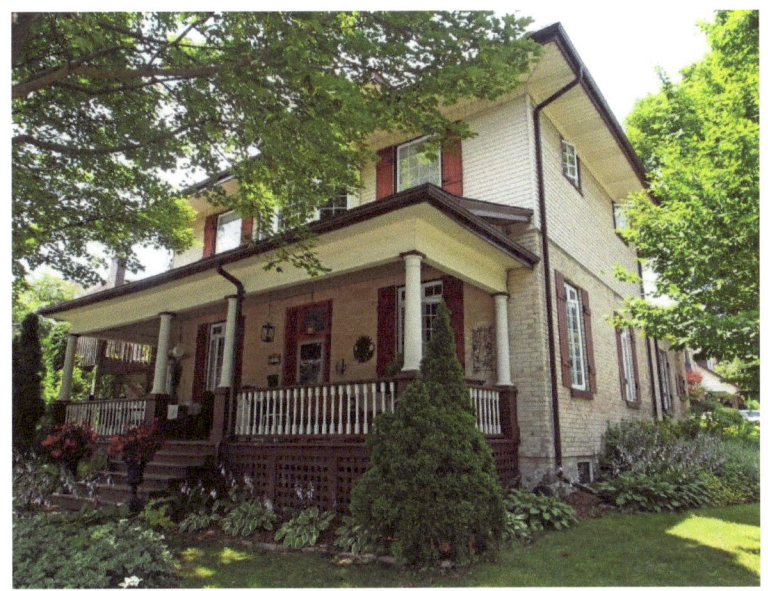

209 Light Street

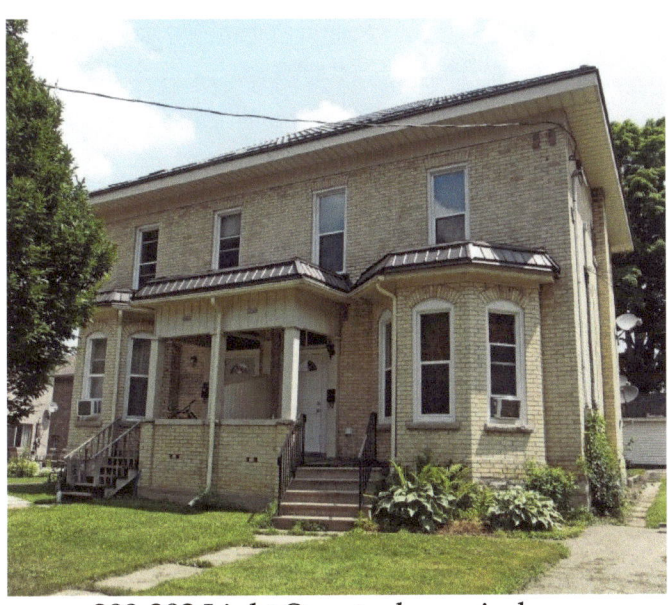

200-202 Light Street – bay windows

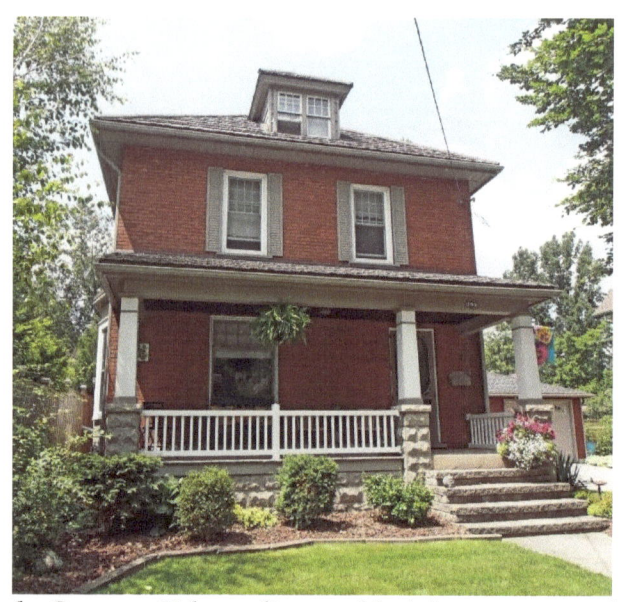

193 Light Street – Edwardian red brick two-storey home – open verandah with tapered Doric posts on large cement piers

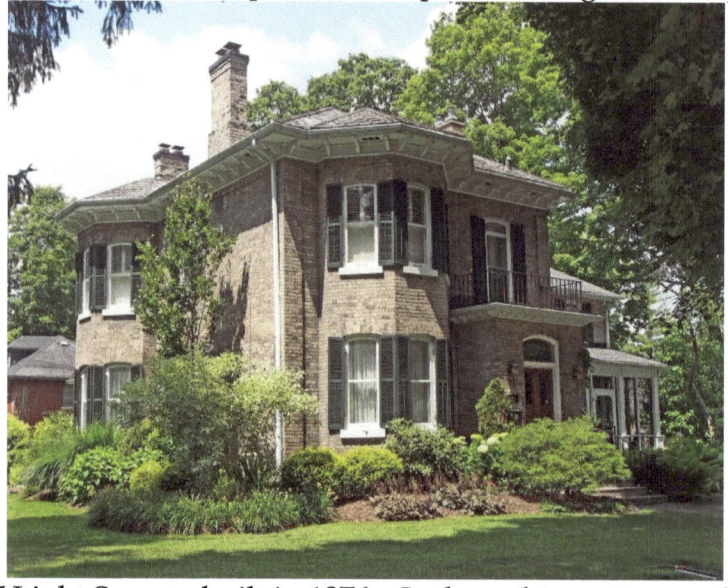

177 Light Street – built in 1876 – L-shaped two-storey white brick house with a grey slate roof with many small cornice brackets; fieldstone foundation, balcony above door

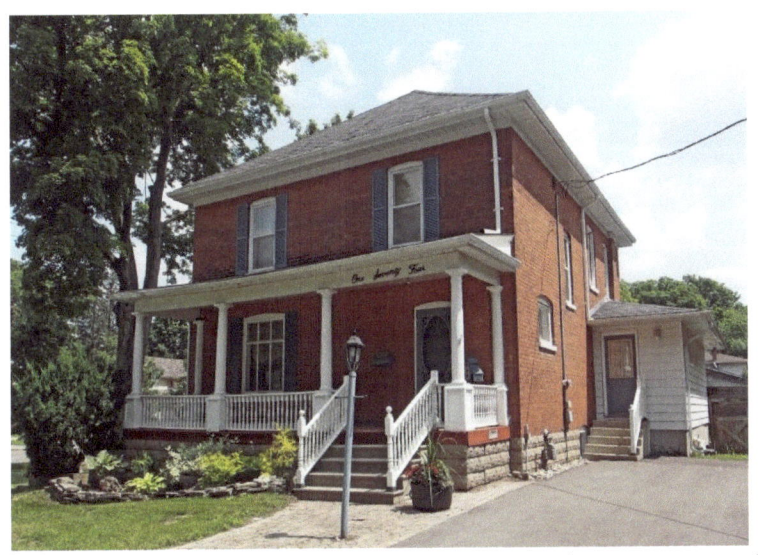

174 Light Street – two-storey Edwardian with open verandah
supported by Doric pillars, hipped roof

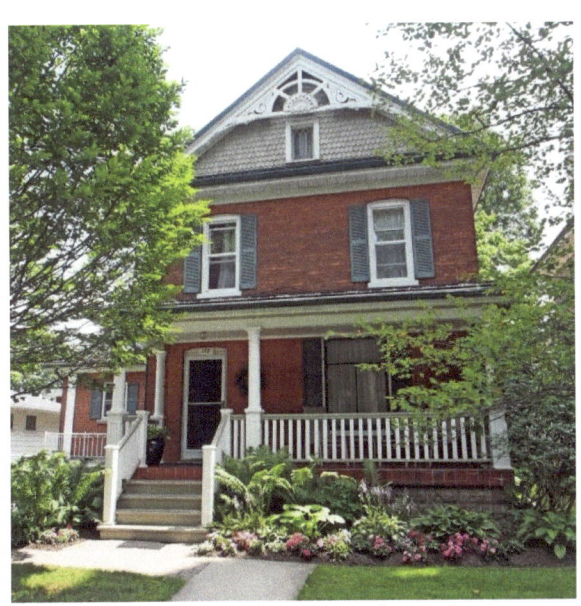

172 Light Street – Gothic, verge board trim on gable

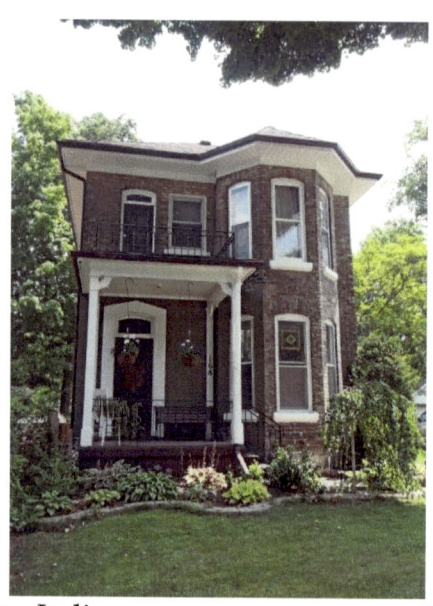

168 Light Street – Italianate, two-storey tower-like bay, second floor balcony

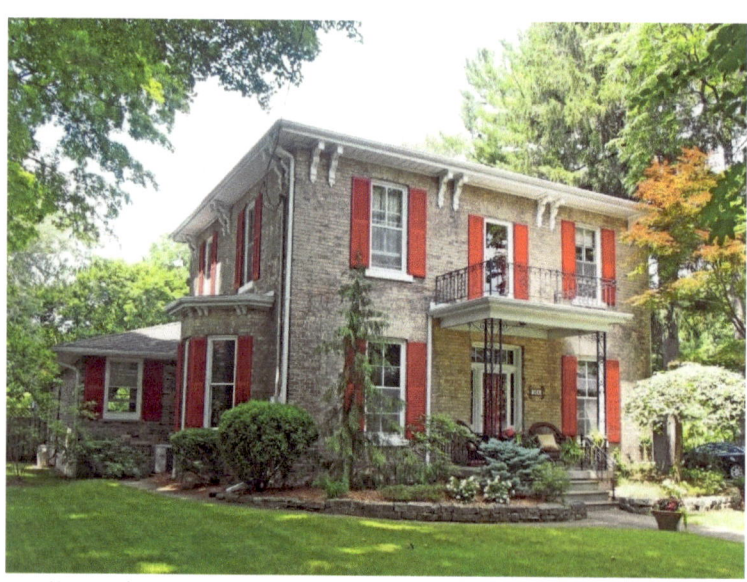

165 Light Street – Italianate, paired cornice brackets

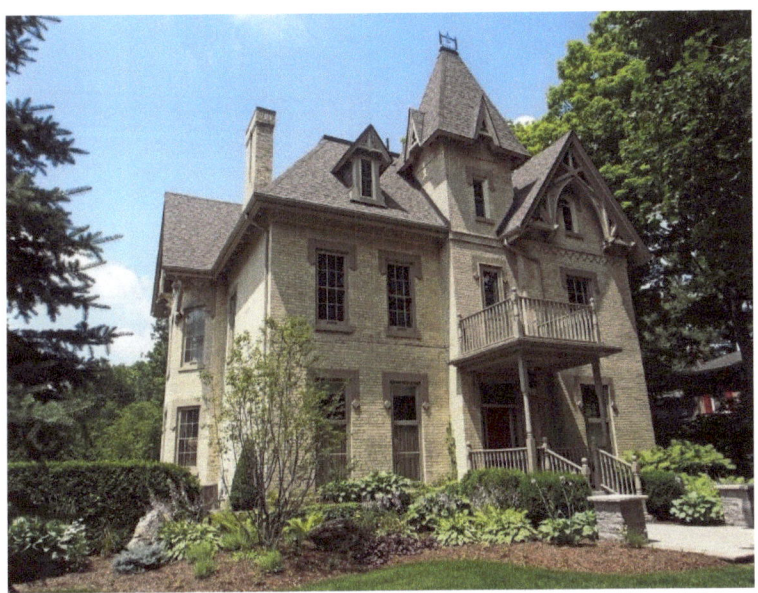

157 Light Street – built in 1875 – Queen Anne style with varied roof line, decorated verge board on gables, dormers and tower; second-floor balcony

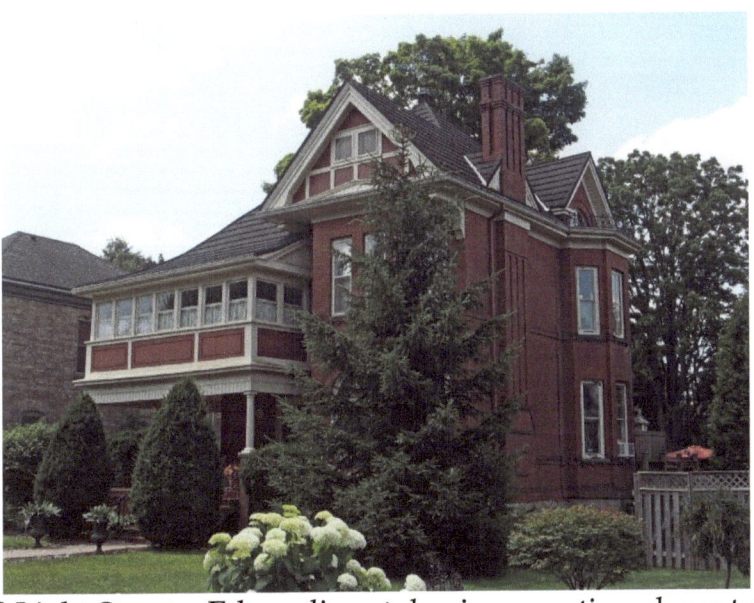

139 Light Street – Edwardian style - iron cresting above two-storey bay window on side, enclosed second floor sunroom

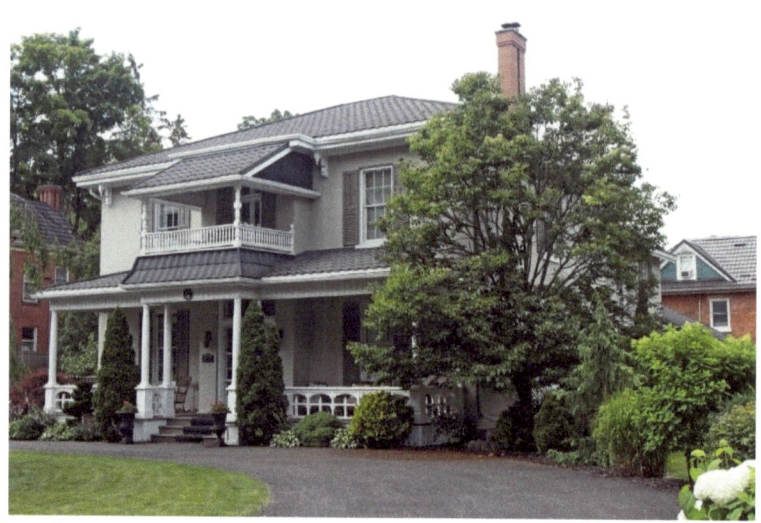

147 Light Street – Neo-Classical symmetrical two-storey home with painted brick; 6/6 double hung windows and decorated shutters; tapered Doric pillars support an open verandah and open balcony; sidelights and transom flank the centered entrance; foundation is cut stone

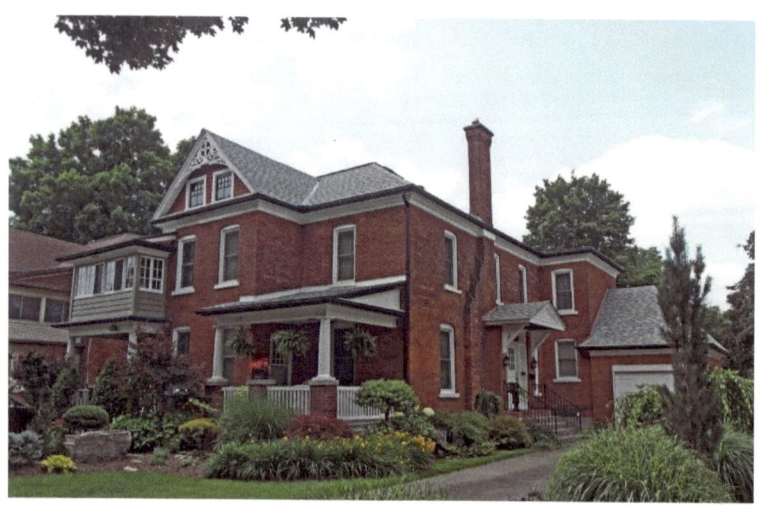

119 Light Street - Edwardian

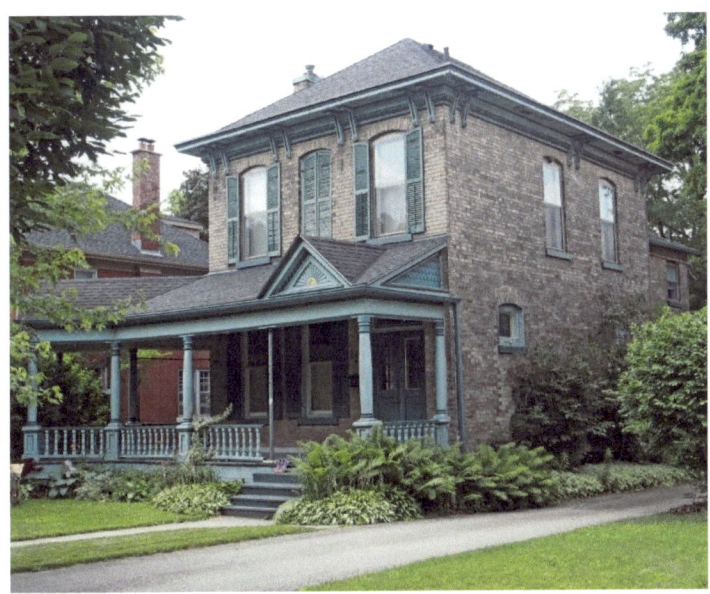

135 Light Street – Italianate, paired cornice brackets, segmented windows, double front doors, and uniquely-shaped verandah supported by Doric pillars; offset section of verandah allowed cooler air to circulate

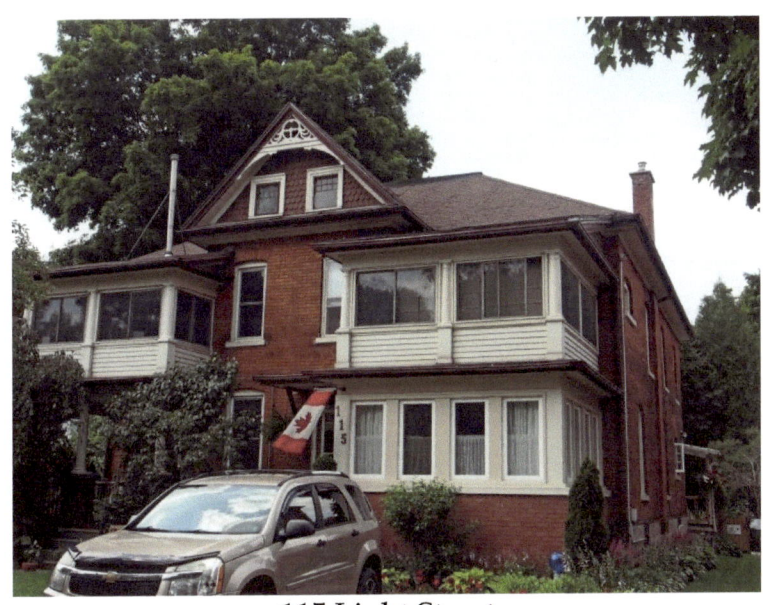

115 Light Street

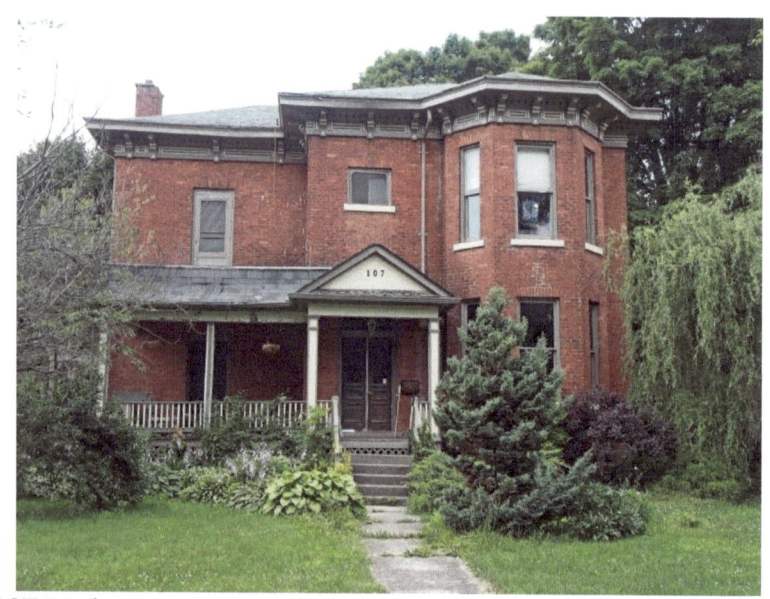

107 Light Street – Italianate, hipped roof, cornice brackets, pediment above door

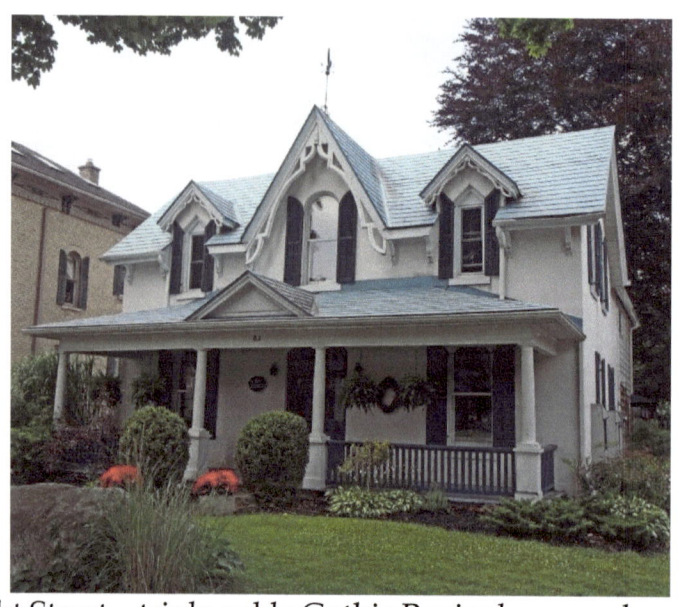

81 Light Street – triple gable Gothic Revival – verge board trim on gables, pediment

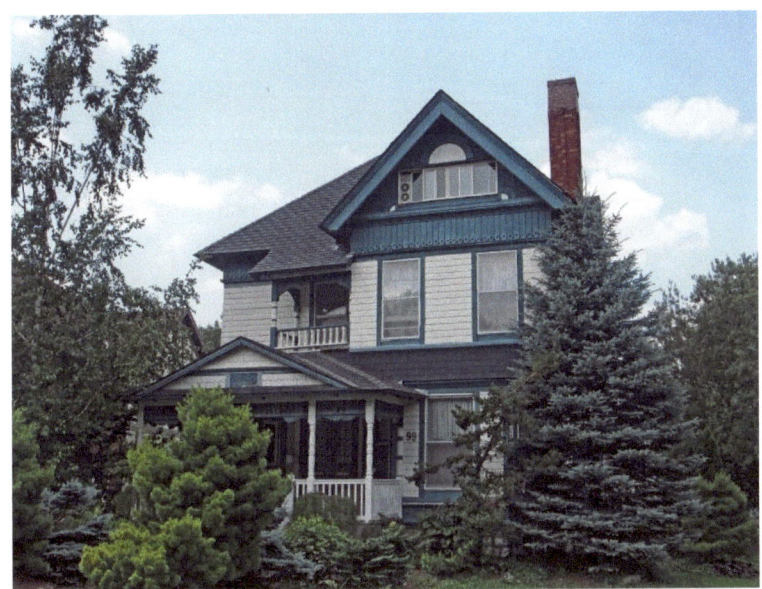

99 Light Street – Queen Anne – two-storey wood-clad home, hip roof with gables; open verandah decorated with brackets and bric-a-brac and supported by Doric columns topped by a small balcony

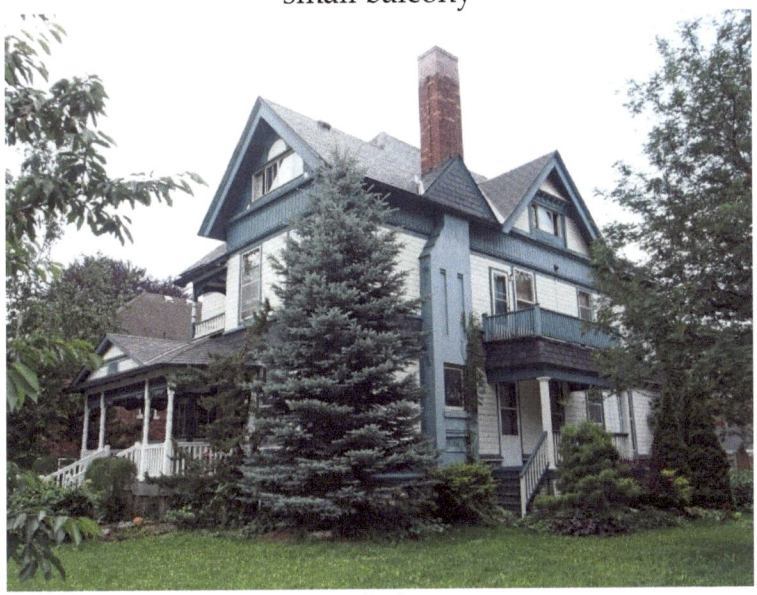

Rear balcony

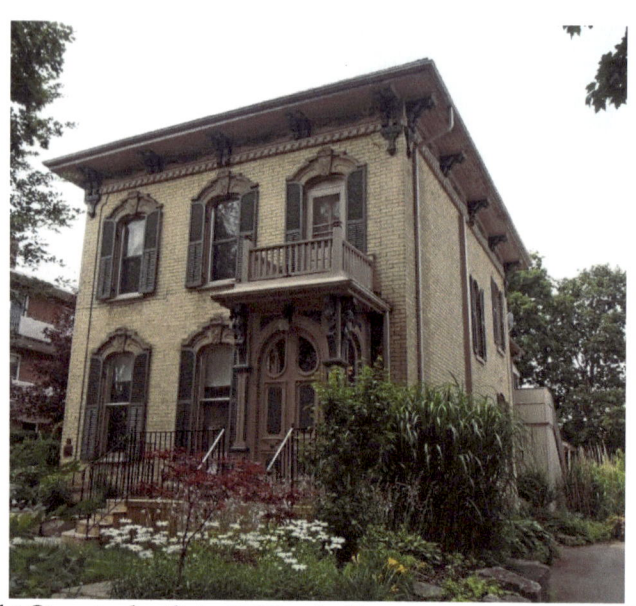

77 Light Street – built in 1878 – Italianate, two-storey buff brick home, cut field stone foundation, decorative cornice with paired brackets and dentils, window hoods with keystones

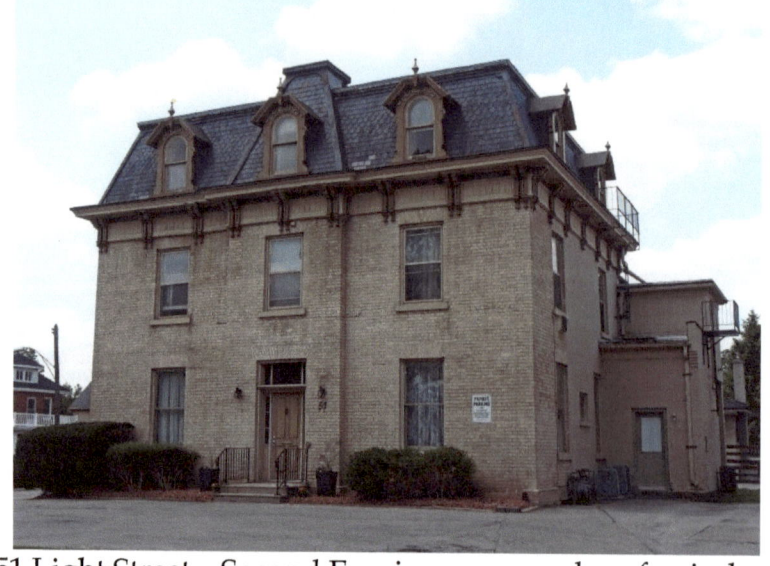

51 Light Street – Second Empire – mansard roof, window hoods, cornice brackets

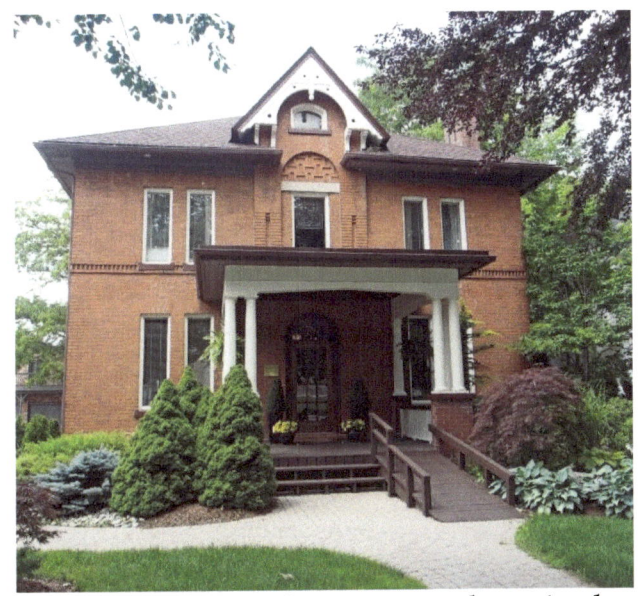

39 Light Street – symmetrical, two-storey plus attic, cleaned red brick, hip roof, centred dormer with verge board and paired brackets; soldier-styled drip course basket weave above central window; paired Doric columns support the open porch

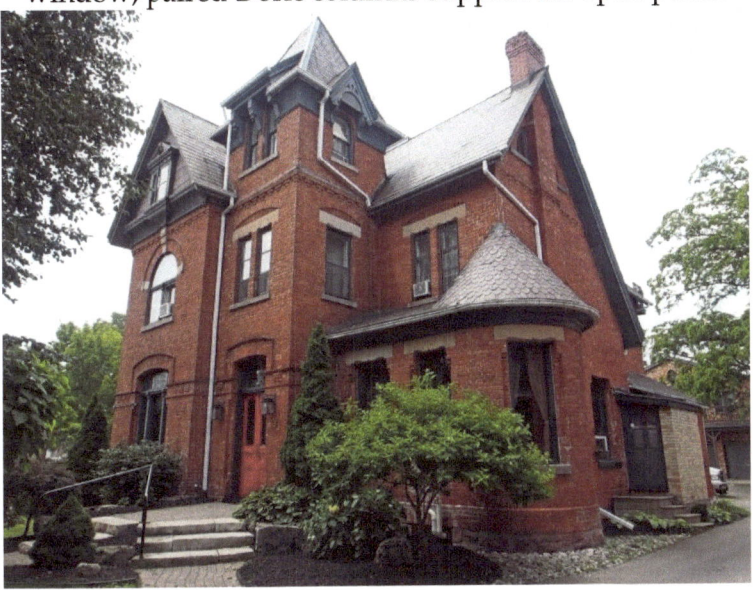

33 Light Street – Queen Anne, turret, three-storey tower

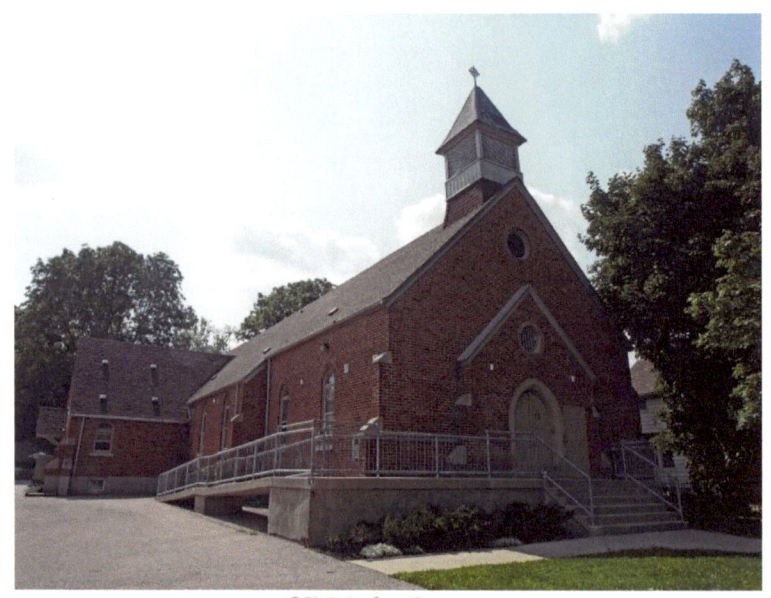

25 Light Street

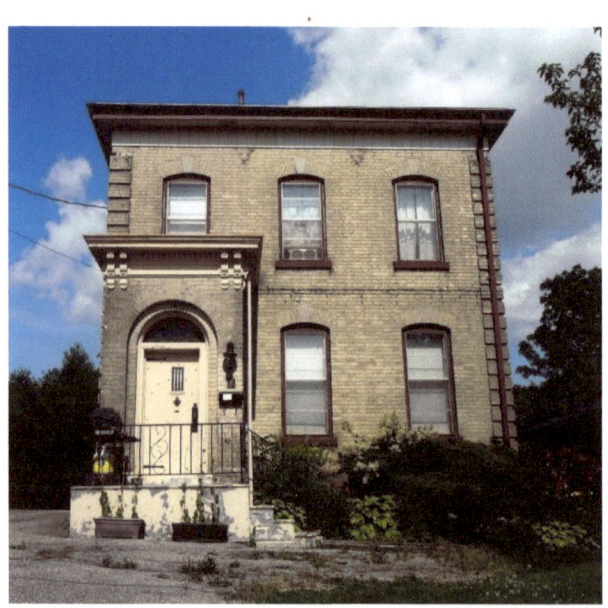

Light Street – Italianate, corner quoins, cornice brackets

Architectural Terms

Banding: Different materials, colors or textures used in horizontal bands along a wall. Example: 399 Drew Street, Page 32	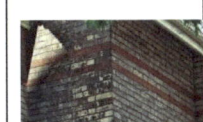
Bay Window: A window that projects out from a wall, in a semicircular, rectangular, or polygonal design. Used frequently in Gothic and Victorian designs. Example: 76 Wellington Street, Page 9	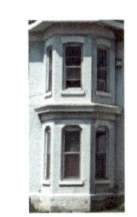
Brackets: a decorative or weight-bearing structural element which forms a right angle with one side against a wall and the other under a projecting surface such as an eave or roof. Example: 62 Wellington Street, Page 8	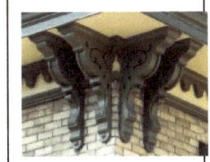
Buttress: a masonry structure built against or projecting from a wall which serves to support or reinforce the wall. In Canadian architecture, they are sometimes used for decoration. Example: 34 Riddell Street, Page 26	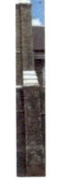

Capital: The uppermost finish or decoration on a column. An Ionic column has a small base, a thin elegant shaft, and a capital composed of volutes which are carved whirls or twists that take the form of a scroll. A Doric column is characterized by a plain column with no base, a shaft with twenty flutings, and a simple capital with a simple entablature. Example: 57 Wellington Street (Ionic) 147 Light Street (Doric), Page 42	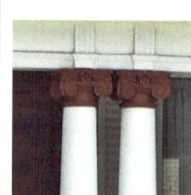 Ionic 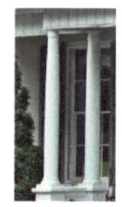 Doric
Cornice: originally the wooden overhang of the roof. With the use of stone, brick, iron and steel, the cornice is any projecting shelf at the top of a ceiling or roof. They can be very decorative. Example: 62 Wellington Street, Page 8	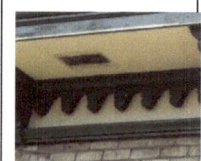
Dentil Moulding: an even series of rectangles used as ornamental decoration in cornices. Example: Riddell Street, Page 23	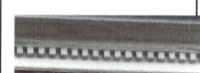
Dichromatic brick/tilework: the use of two colours of brick, tile or slate to decorate a façade. Example: 399 Drew Street, Page 32	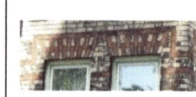
Dormer: (French for "sleep") a gable end window that pierces through the plane of a sloping roof surface to create usable space in the top floor or attic of a building by adding headroom. Example: 70 Wellington Street, Page 18	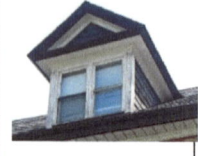

Entrance: The entrance encompasses the doorway and the inner vestibule or, in residential architecture, the covered porch. Example: 59 Riddell Street, Page 28	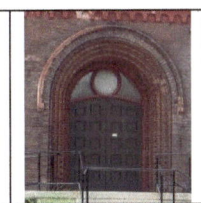
Fretwork: interlaced decorative design resembling a bracket Example: 36 Wellington Street North, Page 14	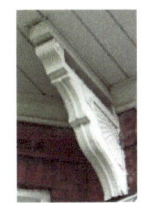
Gable: the triangular portion of a wall between the edges of a sloping roof. Example: 321 Drew Street, Page 34	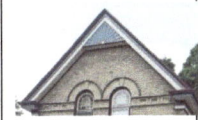
Hipped Roof: a roof where all sides slope downwards to the walls with no gables. Example: 40 Wellington Street South, Page 11	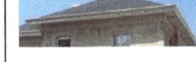
Iron Cresting: A decorative ornament along the top of a roof. Iron cresting was popular in the Baroque era and also in Italianate, Victorian, Second Empire and Queen Anne styles of architecture. Example: 139 Light Street, Page 41	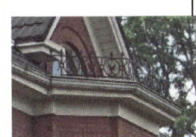
Keystones and Voussoirs: a voussoir is a wedge-shaped element used in building an arch. A keystone is the central stone that locks all the stones into position, allowing the arch to bear weight. A keystone is often enlarged and embellished. Example: 321 Drew Street, Page 34	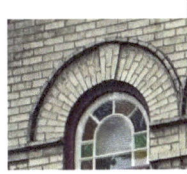

Lancet Window: a tall, narrow window with a pointed arch at its top. Example: 34 Riddell Street, Page 26	
Mansard Roof: This style was popularized by Francois Mansart (1598-1666), an accomplished architect of the French Baroque period and especially fashionable during the Second French Empire (1852-1870). This roof is almost flat on the top section, with two slopes on each of its sides with the lower slope at a steeper angle than the upper and having dormer windows. Example: 51 Light Street, Page 46	
Palladian Window: a large window that is divided into three sections with the centre section larger than the two side sections and usually arched. Example: 49 Wellington Street, Page 16	
Pediment: a triangular section above the horizontal structure (entablature), typically supported by columns. The inside of the triangle is called the tympanum. Example: 20-22 Wellington Street, Page 13	
Quoin: masonry blocks at the corner of a wall, often a decorative feature, usually larger or of a different colour than the rest of the wall. Example: 75 Wellington Street, Page 9	

Rose Window: a circular window with ornamental tracery radiating from the centre. Example: 34 Riddell Street, Page 26	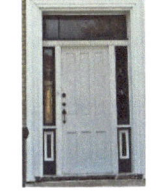
Sidelight: a window, usually with a vertical emphasis, that flanks a door, and is often used to emphasize the importance of a primary entrance. **Transom Window:** the light above the doorway, also called a fanlight. Example: 51 Wellington Street, Page 6	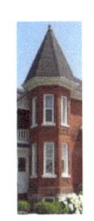
Turret: a small tower that projects from the wall of a building. Example: 36 Wellington Street North, Page 14	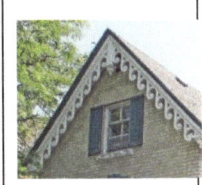
Vergeboard and Finial: also called bargeboards – hang from the projecting end of a roof and are often elaborately carved and ornamented. **Finial:** ornament added to the top of a gable, pinnacle, canopy or spire – a Gothic element. Example: 45 Wellington Street, Page 11	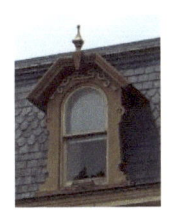
Window Hood: A **hood** is the piece found above window openings, usually of an ornate design, and covers the top third of the opening. Hoods are commonly placed above arched or curved openings on both windows and doors. Example: 51 Light Street, Page 46	

Building Styles

Edwardian, 1900-1930 – This style bridges the ornate and elaborate styles of the Victorian era and the simplified styles of the 20th century. Balanced facades, simple roof lines, dormer windows, large front porches, and smooth brick surfaces are its characteristics. Example: 376 Drew Street, Page 36	
Georgian, before 1860 – This style began with the British King Georges in the 18th century. These buildings have balanced facades around a central door, medium-pitched gable roofs, and small paned windows. Example: 487 Riddell Street, Page 25	
Gothic Revival, 1830-1890 – These decorative buildings have sharply-pitched gables with highly detailed verge boards, pointed-arch window openings, and dichromatic brickwork. It is a common style in Ontario. Example: 81 Light Street, Page 44	
Italianate, 1850-1900 – It has wide-bracketed eaves, belvederes, wrap-around verandahs.

Example: 48 Wellington Street, Page 15 | |

Neo-Classical (1810 - 1850) – This style was a direct result of the War of 1812. Many Upper Canadians returning from the war with the United States were second or third generation Loyalists who had inherited land and means from their forefathers. Once the conflict had passed, they had the money and the time to expand their holdings and indulge their architectural whims. Both residential and commercial buildings were constructed on the traditional Georgian plan, but they had a new gaiety and light-heartedness. Detailing became more refined, delicate, and elegant. Example: 147 Light Street, Page 42	
Queen Anne, 1885-1900 – This style is distinguished by an irregular outline featuring a combination of an offset tower, broad gables, projecting two-storey bays, verandahs, multi-sloped roofs, and tall, decorative chimneys. A mixture of brick and wood is common. Windows often have one large single-paned bottom sash and small panes in the upper sash. Example: 33 Light Street, Page 47	
Regency Cottage, 1830-1860 – This style originated in England in 1815 and spread to Ontario later in the 19th century as British officers retired to Canada. It is a modest one-storey house with a low-pitched hip roof and has a symmetrical front façade. Example: 64 Wellington Street, Page 16	

Saltbox: A saltbox is a building with a long, pitched roof that slopes down to the back, generally a wooden frame house. A saltbox has just one storey in the back and two stories in the front. The asymmetry of the unequal sides and the long, low rear roof line are the most distinctive features of a saltbox, which takes its name from its resemblance to a wooden lidded box in which salt was once kept. The earliest saltbox houses were created when a lean-to addition was added onto the rear of the original house extending the roof line sometimes to less than six feet from ground level. Example: 328 Drew Street, Page 34	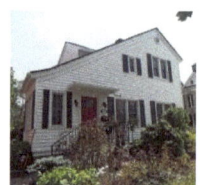
Second Empire, 1860-1880 – The mansard roof is the most noteworthy feature of this style and is evidence of the French origins. Projecting central towers and one or two-storey bays can also be present. Example: 51 Light Street, Page 46	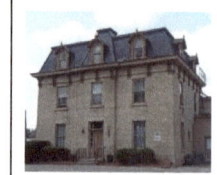
Vernacular/Traditional Mode 1638 - 1950 Influenced but not defined by a particular style, vernacular buildings are made from easily available materials and exhibit local design characteristics. Example: 45 Wellington Street South, Page 11	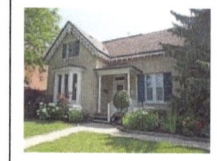

www.ingramcontent.com/pod-product-compliance
Lightning Source LLC
Chambersburg PA
CBHW040857180526
45159CB00001B/448